The 11ᵀᴴ Ḥour:

The Sequel to The 7th Guest

The Official Strategy Guide

Rusel DeMaria
Alex Uttermann

Prima Publishing

Secrets of the Games and logo are registered trademarks of
Prima Publishing, a division of Prima Communications, Inc.

The Prima logo is a trademark of Prima Publishing, a division of
Prima Communications, Inc.

Prima Publishing™ is a trademark of Prima Communications, Inc.

The 7th Guest™, The 11th Hour™, Trilobyte™ are trademarks of Trilobyte, Inc. ©
1993, 1995 Trilobyte, Inc.
Original Concept sketches found between pages 151 and 225 by Robert Stein III.
Photography by Rusel DeMaria, Rob Landeros & Bill McClain.

Project Editor: Kip Ward

ISBN: 1-55958-528-5

Library of Congress Catalog Card Number: 94-66679

95 96 97 98 BB 10 9 8 7 6 5 4 3 2 1

Printed in the United States of America

Created by DeMaria Studio for
Prima Publishing, Rocklin, CA

The 11TH Hour:™

The Sequel to The 7th Guest™

The Official Strategy Guide

Now Available
Computer Game Books

The 7th Guest: The Official Strategy Guide
Alone in the Dark 3: The Official Strategy Guide
Betrayal at Krondor: The Official Strategy Guide
Buried in Time: The Official Strategy Guide
CD-ROM Games Secrets, Volume 1
Celtic Tales: Balor of the Evil Eye--The Official Strategy Guide
Cyberia: The Official Strategy Guide
Descent: The Official Strategy Guide
DOOM II: The Official Strategy Guide
Heretic: The Official Strategy Guide
Kingdom: The Far Reaches--The Official Strategy Guide
King's Quest VII: The Unauthorized Strategy Guide
The Legend of Kyrandia: The Official Strategy Guide
Lode Runner: The Legend Returns--The Official Strategy Guide
Machiavelli the Prince: Official Secrets & Solutions
Marathon: The Official Strategy Guide
Master of Orion: The Official Strategy Guide
Master of Magic: The Official Strategy Guide
Mech Warrior 2: The Official Strategy Guide
Microsoft Space Simulator: The Official Strategy Guide
Myst: The Official Strategy Guide, Revised Edition
The Pagemaster Official CD-ROM Strategy Guide and Companion
PowerHouse Official Secrets and Solutions
Prince of Persia: The Official Strategy Guide
Sid Meier's Civilization, or Rome on 640K a Day
Sid Meier's Colonization: The Official Strategy Guide
SimCity 2000: Power, Politics, and Planning
SimTower: The Official Strategy Guide
Spaceword Ho! Official Secrets and Solutions
Terry Pratchett's Discworld: The Official Strategy Guide
TIE Fighter: The Official Strategy Guide
TIE Fighter: Defender of the Empire--Official Secrets & Solutions
Under a Killing Moon: The Official Strategy Guide
WarCraft: Orcs & Humans Official Secrets & Solutions
X-COM Terror From The Deep: The Official Strategy Guide
X-COM UFO Defense: The Official Strategy Guide
X-Wing Collector's CD-ROM: The Official Strategy Guide

How to Order:
For information on quantity discounts contact the publisher: Prima Publishing, P.O. Box 1260BK, Rocklin, CA 95677-1260; (916) 632-4400. On your letterhead include information concerning the intended use of the books and the number of books you wish to purchase.

CONTENTS

Developer's Word

Your hands tremble. Just slightly. Enough, though, for Stauf to notice. He notices everything. Your hands. Your thoughts. . . . Your soul. It's your move. Your brow furrows—your mind racing, calculating. . . Suddenly, an idea. Yes, yes. Terribly clever, you tell yourself, the thought punctuated by a commanding click. But Stauf knows before you do which move you'll make. He's quick with a reply. And now you've found yourself in quite a bind. Stauf laughs menacingly, taunts you. . . and taunts you again. Why so nervous? you ask yourself, a fainthearted smile playing across your lips. It's. . . just a computer game. . . isn't it?

The 11th Hour improves on *The 7th Guest* in a number of crucial ways. Most importantly, we've sought to draw the player more deeply into the interactive experience and to enhance the illusion that it is with evil Old Man Stauf, and not merely a computer program, that the player actually engages. (It is, after all, an illusion. . . isn't it?) To that end, the player character has been transformed into a corporal entity, and a treasure hunt has been added, thereby better enabling the player to feel his presence within the environment. In addition, the visual presentation has been refined, darkened and rendered more threatening, the setting contemporized, and the characters more fully and compellingly drawn. The story is slicker, sexier and more terrifying. And it's bigger. Much bigger.

The 11th Hour is finally on the shelves and everyone is pretty excited here at Trilobyte. We feel we've come up with another milestone in the CD-ROM industry. *The 11th Hour* is, quite literally, huge: it takes up four times as much disc space as *The 7th Guest.* Our proprietary object-oriented engine creates even faster, more fluid navigation and puzzle play. The full length 11th Hour motion picture runs at thirty frames per second on your home computer (that's just like a video you'd play on your TV). It's the sharpest full motion video playback ever created. *The 11th Hour* has artificial intelligence games that get harder each time you go back and play them again. Our story is more compelling and exciting. The sound is fantastic. We have developed a Gestalt experience that successfully combines technology with creativity, storytelling with game

design. We've put our blood, sweat and years into this splendid beast.
At last, it's ready for you to play.

The Official Strategy Guide

So why should you buy this book? Because we think it's a cool, concise,
accessible companion to our game. It's got hints and solutions, the story
from Carl Denning's point of view, and the complete screenplay to the
movie. *The 11th Hour, the Sequel to the 7th Guest: The Official Strategy
Guide* just adds to the enjoyment of the CD-ROM. You may not believe
this, but almost everyone at Trilobyte has a copy of *The 7th Guest: The
Official Strategy Guide* on their desks. Even we need a little help
sometimes. (By the way, quit complaining about the Microscope puzzle
from *The 7th Guest*. Graeme, the designer, says it's cinchy.)

   And, of course, you'll also find here, much to Stauf's dismay, solutions
to all those treacherous brain teasers of which he is so deliciously fond.
All except for one, that is. At the conclusion of *The 11th Hour*, every
player is asked to solve one final "puzzle." It's a riddle solved not with the
logical mind, but with the heart, the body, and the conscience—a moral
dilemma, if you will. It's a decision each player must make on his own,
the consequences of which he'll bear for the rest of his life. We trust you'll
choose wisely. Stauf, of course, trusts otherwise. . .

   Finally, we suggest you keep this book hidden from Stauf. The prospect
of defeat angers him, to say the least, and his wrath has been known to
carry, well. . . unpredictable consequences. But, otherwise, enjoy.

Finally, a Little Advice.

Here is a WARNING. If you do buy this book, don't use it like a crutch
or you'll miss out. There are logical solutions to all the puzzles in
Stauf's mansion. We, as game designers, honor fair play, and our
programmers thrive on logic. So even though Stauf is a crazy, capricious
maniac, when it comes to his games, he's about as honest and fair as a
trickster and thief can be. Only use the strategy guide when you are
stuck in the deepest rut, when you're so wound up by Stauf's nasty
taunts that you feel like throwing your monitor out the window. Sit
back, take a deep breath, reach for your *Official Strategy Guide*. Pretend
you're a sorcerer's apprentice stealing a glance in the magician's secret
book. Read one of the hints for that "impossible" puzzle in the
Walkthrough section, then try and solve it again on your own.

Whatever you do, don't skip ahead to the Solutions if you can restrain yourself! The more you play on your own, the more you use your throbbing brain, the cleverer you become.

Then, when you've finished the game once or twice, you might like to return to the story and read the whole Walkthrough to get a little more inside Carl's head. Ooohh. Bad move. . .

Oh, and one final bit of advice. Do be careful what you wish for.

©1994 Bill McClain

Graeme and Rob
Medford, 1994

INTRODUCTION

Welcome back to Stauf's place. It's still not a cheery place, but this time everybody does know your name. Espcially Stauf and his ghostly friends. Now, years later, you get to play Carl Denning, intrepid TV reporter in search of your lost producer and sometime lover, Robin. In these pages, we'll tried to show you how you (Carl) can defeat Stauf and, well, come out alive.

The first part of the book is a fictionalized walkthrough that takes you through the entire game, from start to finish. This is one possible scenario. There are other ways to play the game—for instance, solving puzzles in a different order—so you shouldn't feel that this is the only one. Still, this is a fairly logical approach to *The 11th Hour* and it will get you as far as you want to go. The Walkthrough is divided into chapters, each chapter dealing with a particular hour (module) and the treasure hunts and puzzles associated with that section of the game. However, the Walkthrough does not step you through all the puzzles. It mostly gives hints about how to solve them. Complete solutions come later.

The second part of this book contains the original script, as written by Trilobyte, and essentially unedited. We thought you would like to see what this game looked like before it became a game.

The third part of the book is a very condensed guide through the game that we've called the Quick Walkthrough. This gives you a no-frills approach to the flow of the game and the order in which you might best solve the puzzles and find the little "treasures" Stauf sets out for you.

The fourth part of the book is the solution section. In this section, you'll find solutions for all the puzzles, sometimes more than one. We've done our best to offer strategies for the artificial intelligence puzzles (there are no real solutions), but we can't guarantee that you won't need to have some of them solved for you. Sorry.

After the puzzle solutions is an interview with Graeme Devine and Rob Landeros, the two principal developers of both *The 7th Guest* and *The 11th Hour.*

Finally, there's an index of treasure hunts and puzzles.

So have fun, and good luck. Stauf is back. . . .

Authors'
Acknowledgments

Thanks to all the people at Trilobyte. . . the list is long. . . for all your help. Special thanks to Graeme and Rob, of course. Special scratches under the chin for Scruffy@tbyte.com.

   Also to all the folks at Prima for hanging in there in the face of danger, and to Kip Ward in particular for being cool.

   As a profound aside; thanks, Trilobyte, for being in Medford, OR - just close enough to Ashland for us to have rediscovered Aletheia.

THE 11ᵀᴴ HOUR

THE STORY

Connecticut is where I'm not Carl Denning—not the celebrity TV reporter everyone recognizes. Here, I'm just a regular guy. Connecticut is where I find peace of mind. The outside world doesn't intrude, and my private life is my own when I'm holed up in the country.

Then I got involved with Robin Morales, the producer of my show, Case Unsolved, and after her strange disappearance in Upstate New York, even my country retreat couldn't keep the public away. All of a sudden, my affair with her was a subject for the evening news, dished up for anyone with a TV to watch.

Robin's headstrong curiosity about the strange mansion of Henry Stauf had begun to intrude more and more into our daily lives, as she vacillated between her desire to find out more about the mansion and her repulsion and fright at the few gory details she'd managed to gather. To my untrained eye, she was obsessed with Stauf, and I didn't much like it. Then she left. Her head was filled with fearful stories of guests dying off around Stauf in the 1920s; she had told me enough of them. And there was a legacy of myths about visitors to the mansion who never returned.

I, too, had absorbed more than my share of lore about the Stauf Mansion and its demonic legend. At the time, I was resentful, but in retrospect, that unintentional knowledge may have saved my life.

She took off to investigate what she kept saying could be the story of a lifetime. It scared her to no end, especially in light of recent murders in that area, and yet she was gripped in the fascination of the "haunted" Stauf Mansion. The story of a lifetime. How little we both knew then about the twisted truth of that statement!

I hadn't heard from Robin at all for a few weeks, after she left for Harley-on-Hudson. Not so much as a word from her. Perhaps that's not altogether surprising, as we'd more or less broken up right before she left. But I don't want to talk about that just yet.

This strange and disturbing tale of mine needs to be told from the beginning. It's true enough that my feelings for Robin are a significant part of the story, but as it turns out, that part pales when compared to the bizarre and ghoulish chain of events her disappearance triggered. The memory of that time is still enough to make my blood run cold. That's why I try not to think about any of it at all.

Once it was all over, I certainly had no desire to do any show about that horrid mansion near the Hudson River. Yet, as time passes, I feel a need to tell the whole story, once and for all, as a way to get rid of my personal demons connected with it.

Perhaps readers have something to learn from my story about the ghosts of grief, arrogance and greed. Maybe they feel, as I did, that they have nothing left to learn in this life. If that's the case, I pity them from the bottom of my heart, for it is with that kind of cocky, self-satisfied arrogance that I began the horrendous journey to Harley-on-Hudson and saw, heard and experienced tragic and ghastly events which no human should ever see or hear or experience. My arrogance has long disappeared.

I am truly grateful for my life, and hope that by the end of my tale, readers will understand just how lucky I am to be able to write these words.

Carl Denning
Connecticut, 1995

CHAPTER ONE

The Leave-Taking

Robin was gone. She had broken up with me, trying to preserve her professional reputation as my producer. We had quarreled, and she had gone away to lick her wounds, in Harley-on-Hudson, of all the god-forsaken places on the planet.

"Well, maybe if I'm lucky, you'll become another missing person in Harley," I'd snapped at her during our fight. How I wished those bitter words unsaid, now!

I was sitting in my living room when the formal announcement came over the news. The State Police had called off the search for Robin. They'd simply decided that she'd disappeared for good and would never be found. Just written her off with a shrug as one more missing person, the bastards, and

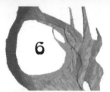

gone on to some other, more important case.

The idiotic news anchor mentioned that Robin's disappearance was possibly connected with the recent murders in the Hudson Valley. In my mounting rage and frustration, even I knew that was probably true—but I didn't want to believe it. I've heard a lot about people having regrets when someone dies, about the important things that are forever unresolved, gnawing at their souls long after the person was gone. I didn't want to think that I'd never say "I really love you, and I'm sorry" to a living, breathing Robin Morales.

I turned off the television once the news story got to showing my own ugly mug—talking about Robin and me as an item. I didn't need to hear that again.

Just then the doorbell rang. The sound startled me, as did the small package waiting for me on the doorstep. A delivery truck drove away as I noticed the small box carried no return address. I assumed I was just jittery because of the news report, and thinking about Robin, but I had a really creepy feeling as I carefully opened the mystery package.

There was a small computer inside, like one of the personal data things people carry, or one of those little game things kids play with. When I looked at the small screen, I saw—I know this doesn't sound real, but believe it, I really did see—Robin's face. She cried out to me in a voice that broke my heart.

"Carl . . help me . . . please! I can't get out!" she called and then the screen went blank. Was this some kind of a ransom notice? A sick joke? It just didn't make any sense.

I tried pushing the little buttons, but nothing happened. The screen stayed dead. I tossed the little computer on top of the TV, and paced the room. What was this? What did it mean? Was Robin, obviously in trouble, trying to tell me something?

Frustration and fear battled it out in my chest. I felt completely helpless. Focusing my thoughts on where Robin might be, and on how I was going to find her, didn't help all that much. I wanted to do something. I was lost in thought when the little computer started beeping.

I picked it up again, a little uncertain that I wanted anything to do with this strange machine, and the little screen lit up. The image was an old rambling house. I recognized it instantly as the Stauf Mansion. Robin had shown me plenty of pictures of the place. This was getting creepier by the minute. Was Robin in the house somewhere? I thought back over what she'd said—"I can't get out!"—it didn't make a lot of sense that she couldn't get out of an old house. Unless something—or someone—was keeping her there. I shuddered.

I looked back at the screen, but it had gone black again. "Damn!" I spat the word. Those images had to come back! I needed to know what to do next. Was this screen showing me reality, or was it some psycho joke? Or both? If Robin was still alive. . . I swallowed hard. That's when her face came back on the screen. She looked terrible. Frightened. "Help me. . ." she pleaded.

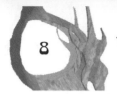

I didn't need any more proof that this was Robin, alive, but in terrible danger. I ran out of the house, jumped on my motorcycle and went speeding down the road before I even had the time to consider my actions, or where I was going. I had the little computer stuffed in the pocket of my jacket. I had to do something. I couldn't just sit in this rural peace and twiddle my thumbs. I was going to the mansion to get Robin back. Or that was my plan, such as it was.

I drove through southern Connecticut while there was still daylight. Although my trip took me through forest and scenic areas, I was oblivious to anything except the road in front of me. As I sped along the highways, images of Robin and me were running through my mind, like a videotape of a movie I'd seen a hundred times already, but that wouldn't stop playing.

There we were in the city, in that little espresso bar close to the station. We used to go over to grab a bite between filming and production meetings, as colleagues and collaborators on any show would do. It was harmless. For a while. But as things started heating up between Robin and me. . . well, our discussions in that little bar took on the forbidden tension of an affair about to happen.

Both of us had clear ethics about not going out with co-workers. Robin especially had some strong thing against it. I guess because she

was a woman in a mostly male work environment, I don't really know. Maybe it was too threatening to her career, if people talked. But as time went on and our attraction grew. . .

Even though I was riding my motorcycle at break-neck speed down some Connecticut highway, my memories of Robin overwhelmed me. I could clearly hear our conversation over the roar of the engines and see her face against the landscape, as though the scene were playing right before my eyes. My heart was pounding in anticipation, all over again—

I recalled the day when a coffee break could no longer contain our personal relationship.

I heard myself proudly proclaiming how I had a rule about not getting involved with co-workers, and Robin provocatively confirming that she had the same rule. The tension between us was so thick you could have sliced it with a butter knife. Neither of us wanted to play by our own rules, yet we were each waiting for the other to admit it first.

Finally, I came up for air, unable to stand the tension any more. She was so beautiful, so smart, so sexy. And I was horny as hell. She just had that effect on me.

I'd said, "I'm kinda thinking about breaking this rule."

I wasn't exactly surprised when Robin responded quietly, "So am I."

I drove on and on, memories of Robin and me a constant theme, a torment. As it was nearing twilight, I crossed into the state of New York, near Brewster, and headed for the Taconic Parkway. It would take me straight up New York State, not so far from the Hudson River. I was only a few hours, now, from Harley-on-Hudson. I wondered grimly what I would find there.

As I sped along the hills and valleys and slithering curves of the Taconic Parkway, images of my affair with Robin persisted. Bitterly, I recalled the night she'd broken it off with me in that damned New York espresso bar.

She'd cried. It rips me up inside when a woman cries. In my experience, though, often as not it's because I'm breaking up with them. But she was breaking up with me, so I was ripped up, all right, but I was also pissed off. How come she was the one crying, when she was the one breaking up with me? If it hurt her that much, why couldn't we just stay together?

"I just can't go on like this," she'd said. "People . . . everyone thinks I got to be your producer by sleeping with you."

As if that were going to change if she'd suddenly stopped sleeping with me? What did she want from me, anyway? And since when did she care so much about what other people thought?

I shrugged, hurt.

"So . . . didn't you?" I'd asked sarcastically. It's an automatic reaction, I guess. A sort of macho defense mechanism. I fully expected her to slap me, which in some way would have been preferable. But she crumpled instead, and I actually relished the sight of her pain. Good, now she was really hurting, I thought. Like me.

"How can you say that? You of all people. . . You know I'm a good producer." Her voice was soft and reproachful, but I knew I'd hit her where it counts.

"You're good at a lot of things, Robin," I countered. I'd gotten pretty damned tired of bolstering up her ego—and I wasn't about to do it for her again, especially not when she was telling me she was breaking up a good thing because of "what other people thought."

"Carl, I'm sorry. . ." Choked with tears, she was barely able to speak.

Then she sort of ran out of steam, and I jumped in. I'd been frozen in my anger—anger at her, as well as anger at myself for listening to all this crap. I had to save face. In my profession, image is everything. I couldn't let her see me as a simpering fool.

With an effort, I managed, "I'll tell you what, Ms. Morales, I'll just see you in the office on Monday." That was said in my coldest tone of voice, full of the venom of my hard feelings, and I placed special emphasis on the word "Ms.".

"No . . ." she replied. Was she trying to salvage what was left of her dignity? "I'll be in Harley-on-Hudson next week."

""Well, maybe if I'm lucky, you'll become another missing person in Harley." Ha, my final jab at her.

There wasn't much to say after that. Even now, as the scene played itself out in my mind, I could feel my anger at Robin rising up from the pit of my stomach once again. The night air whooshed around me, getting colder as I rode on. For a moment, I wondered why I was following her tracks now. She'd rejected me, humiliated me, left me. And now that she was in some kind of trouble, she wanted me to bail her out. Why should I bother?

The truth was that I regretted what I'd said. Robin Morales was in a great deal of trouble; she needed me. I was going to help Robin because I loved her. She'd called my name in that dark place, crying out for help. I knew in my heart that, deep down, she loved me, too. Maybe now she'd know it. I'd rescue her and she'd forget what "other people thought" and just follow her heart.

Don't laugh. That's really what I was thinking at the time.

Downtown Harley-on-Hudson was little more than a cluster of buildings with a few homes scattered here and there. By blind instinct, I hung a sharp left off of Main Street and drove down a dank, dark road that led me to the fields.

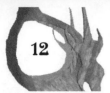

Suddenly, the silhouette of a huge house loomed ahead, blotting out the stars. My skin crawled as I recognized the front gate from Robin's photos. I didn't need to read the name on it to recognize that I had arrived at the Stauf Mansion.

I went through the gate, up to the stairs of the darkened house. I thought of calling out for Robin, but then thought better of it. The whole scene was freakishly quiet, as if the house itself was waiting in anticipation. I just wanted to get in, find Robin, and get out. Quickly.

I reached for the doorknob, but it wouldn't turn in my hand. It seemed to be frozen solid, suffering some result of age and disuse. It was too dark to see. I stood there, a little dumbfounded. For some reason, after riding for all these miles, I expected just to waltz in, find Robin tied up in a closet somewhere, and sashay out again. It was all worked out in my head. Being stopped at the front door didn't figure into my plan at all.

Then I remembered the computer in my pocket. As I pulled it out and opened it, the following words appeared on the screen: "The Blind Mice is a good rap number."

What in the hell was that supposed to mean? And then the stupid thing beeped at me again. Where were these words coming from? Was someone sending them to me? But why? I didn't have a clue.

Or did I? A clue. Some kind of game. A deadly game! Three! Three blind mice! Rap! Knock! I thought I understood. So I rapped on the door three times. And then it opened, with a great rusty squeaking of hinges. At least I'd had the presence of mind to bring a flashlight. I fished it out of my pocket, turned it on, swallowed my fear . . . and walked right into the Stauf Mansion.

CHAPTER TWO

Seven O'Clock

As I stumbled around in the dark, my eyes gradually acclimated to the dim, disk-like patch of light from the flashlight. I found myself in a cavernous entry hall. A loud gong rang seven times, a slow, mournful cadence. Was it a clock? After the last tolling of the gong, the room settled into a deep, and, I thought, natural silence. The air was musty and dank, as though this room had been untouched for decades.

The emptiness was creepy, and the silence so profound that my heart skipped when the electronic machine in my pocket beeped again. I jumped a bit, then ignored it. I turned immediately to the door I had come in and tried to get out, but it wouldn't open. I heard a

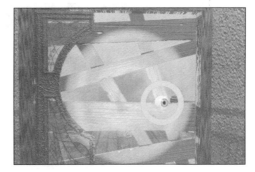

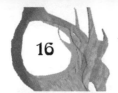

sadistic, cruel laughter and my blood ran cold. I couldn't leave, so I did the next best thing. I opened the GameBook. Another clue appeared, this time spoken in a ghostly male voice that scared me silly for a moment.

Winter coat worn for a mixer?

I was thoroughly confused. What was that supposed to mean? I knew a mixer to be a party. . . I touched the "help" option on the top of the screen, and heard a woman's voice speak the next clue.

Be warned that "worn" means destroyed.

I was still confused, and again touched the help button. I was rewarded with this hint:

Mixer might not be a party. What if it's a beverage?

"Well, then," I thought to myself, "it's a destroyed beverage of some sort." But what did this have to do with finding Robin?

The next hint, *Something's mixed up here.* But what? and the one that followed, *A beverage might be found in the Library,* didn't clear up my mind too much. But at least now I had a place to go looking for something.

There was a button labelled "Map" on the keyboard. I pressed it and was rewarded with a crude diagram of the first floor of the mansion. I

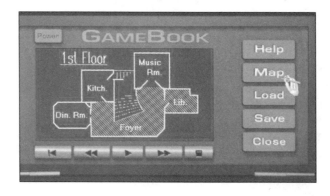

figured out where I was standing, and found that the Library was the first door to the right of the great stairway. OK. I'll play along, I thought. I'll go to the Library.

I got a couple more clues on my way to the Library, moving slowly and cautiously as I went.

Winter coat is an anagram.

Winter coat is an anagram of "Tonic Water".

I closed the GameBook.

Once in the Library, I searched the room, which contained a strange collection of objects—an old brass telescope, a decrepit globe, a painting, books, and other things.

I looked at the books first, curious. The books were red and green, alternating. The GameBook told me to put all the red books on one side and the green books on the other, in four moves. By God, it was a puzzle! The funny thing is, I forgot momentarily the situation I was in. Actually, I kind of enjoy puzzles from time to time. I went about solving the little teaser.

If that was the best they had to offer, I figured I'd breeze through this little mental obstacle course, or whatever it was. Of course, I had no way

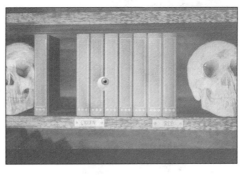

of knowing that this was, in fact, truly nothing more than a teaser. There was much worse to come, as the male voice I had heard before warned.

"You'll not find the next one so pleasant," he taunted.

With a start, I remembered where I was and why I had come.

Robin . . . And yes the tonic water. Something on the fireplace mantle caught my eye, so I went to have a closer look. As I touched the bottle of tonic water, the GameBook seemed to spring to life, and showed me a frozen image of a blonde woman in what appeared to be a restaurant.

As if in a dream, I pushed the 'play' button on the GameBook and watched in horror as Robin, in a pair of dark glasses, came into the diner.

"Just sit anywhere, honey. Menus are on the table." That was the blonde waitress. As she picked up her pad, I could see that she had a prosthetic hand. I didn't mean to, but I shuddered. I wondered if Robin had noticed it, too.

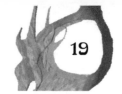

Just at that moment, the video cut off. What did this mean? Where was the video coming from? It was saved, somehow, in the GameBook, and I discovered that I could replay it as many times as I wished. But try as I might, I couldn't get the stupid machine to play any more of that tape. It would only play that little piece and then stop.

I thought about just dashing off through the house looking for Robin. I didn't like participating in this perverse little game. But I decided to play it cool a little while longer, until I learned more.

I was anxious to test my theory of the "game," and started to look around the Library once more.

Immediately, the GameBook beeped again. Another cryptic message.

Rolling rock, bottle cap.

I knew that Rolling Rock was a kind of beer, drank it myself occasionally. But I pressed the help key and heard the reassuring female voice say, "It's a rolling rock bottle cap."

Great. What was the point?

Rolling might mean turmoil. Well, she was right there.

Rock must be another anagram. It sure seemed as though there were a lot of anagrams around here!

Of course, rock is an anagram of cork.

So I was looking for a cork, wasn't I? Even a cork in turmoil, hmm. I hadn't seen a cork just lying around anywhere, so far, in the house. What did I really know about this place? Snatches of conversations with Robin came back to me, about the weird history of the Stauf Mansion, and guests who'd been here before, in the 20s. I'd even read one of the accounts of the goings-on in the house, at Robin's urging. Some of the

guests had been pretty wild, as I recalled, and several of them drank heavily. Anyone who drank heavily might have left a cork around, huh?

It was at this point that I made a key discovery about the Map in the GameBook. Some areas were blank. Others were drawn over with diagonal hatch lines. Then there was the Library. The first time I had looked at it in the Map, it had been hatched. Now it was solid blue. What was the significance of that? Had something I'd done changed the way the Library appeared in the Map?

Finding this Map, which seemed to chronicle my steps in the Stauf Mansion, made me wonder who was watching my every move. I preferred to think it was friend, not foe. Still, there were two voices speaking to me—one male and one female. Could it be that I had a friend and a foe?

I consulted the Map in the GameBook, and saw that the room of Brian Dutton was cross-hatched, on the second floor. Perhaps the mysterious cork might be found there?

Before I left, I looked around at some of the other items in the Library, but every time I tried to touch something, the mysterious, ghostly voice would throw taunts

at me. Finally, I left and returned to the Foyer, then headed toward the stairs leading to the second floor.

I have to admit, my heart was in my throat as I climbed those stairs, and I found myself looking carefully for any missing steps. Creeping around in this empty mansion with nothing but a flashlight and this

Gamer's Note:

Here's a shortcut to the top of the stairs from the Library. Click where you see the hand in the picture, then click the right mouse button to move instantly to the end of the path.

sinister computer to guide me, I wondered why I hadn't waited until daylight to come in here.

The steps were old and shrouded in such darkness that it was difficult to tell exactly where I was stepping. It was a real relief when I made it safely to the second floor. I stood for a moment in front of a painting, a still life of some flowers and fruits. Maybe it was silly of me, but I had a feeling on the nape of my neck, as if unseen eyes were watching me. Heading down the hall to my left, to Dutton's Room, I actually looked back over my shoulder a few times.

Upon entering Brian Dutton's old room, I saw something on the floor. At first, I thought it might be the cork, but on closer inspection, it turned out to be nothing more than a stray lightbulb. Before I could look around for the cork, something else caught my eye. There, in the corner, just to the right of the bulb on the floor, was an old-fashioned cash register, with 162 00 displayed on it. I remembered that Dutton had been sort of greedy about money,

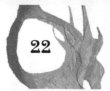

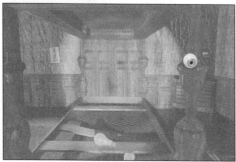

and it was clear to me that this was yet another peculiar puzzle to solve, but what could it mean?

I pressed a few keys on the register, and watched the numbers change. They didn't seem to change in any relation to the numbers I pressed. Or did they?

As I opened the GameBook to look for any hints, I heard again the taunting voice of a man. "You just can't make it add up!"

Somehow I had the sudden intuition that this voice belonged to none other than Henry Stauf! How that could be, considering that Stauf had lived here over 70 years ago, I had no idea. Yet, I knew it was his voice, and it gave me a chill. Although I was kind of a pawn in this game of his, I found I was more truly frightened for Robin.

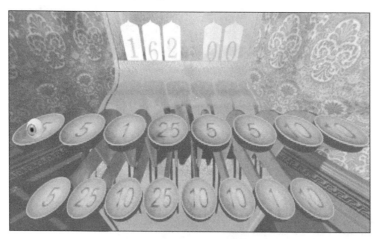

Well, I thought to myself, I'd better figure all of this out in a hurry, so I can get to her. . . before he does.

The first hint about the cash register made sense to me. Divide the keys into two halves of the same shape. In fooling around with the keys, I'd already noticed that the numbers on the display, though they looked

like ordinary dollar amounts, were missing a decimal point, and seemed to have independent relations to the keys. The two numbers on the right side seemed to move together, and the three numbers on the left did, too. Dividing the keys into two halves seemed to support this observation about how the numbers were displayed.

Each half must contain the same amount of money. Huh? I didn't quite follow that one! There were three numbers on the left and two on the right. Unless I had this all wrong, there was no way they would both show the same amount. Maybe Stauf was right, I couldn't make it add up. Unless. . . unless the numbers on the left could be reduced to a number composed of two digits, not three! Hmm. It felt as though I were on to something, but what would that number be?

It seemed that there were too many possible choices between 10 and 99. The next clue filled me in on the additional details. The amount needed in each half is eighty-one cents. Rather than waste my time wondering why this number had arbitrarily been chosen, I went to work. As I pressed the keys, I noticed that each number pressed was subtracted from the left side and added to the right. I also discovered that if I pressed twice on the same key, I could undo my move.

This can't be all that hard, then, I thought. Just think, Carl. I started with the number 10 on the top row, all the way to the right. 152 10, the numbers read out. I pressed the next 10, just to the left of the first one. 142 20, said the cash register. I was really on to something, I knew it. I pressed the five next to the two 10s on the top row. 137 25.

Hmm. I looked at the numbers left on the top row, and decided to switch to the lower one. On the lower row, I again went to the number 10 on the right hand side. 127 35. Whew. I was almost there. I continued to work on the bottom row, until the numbers read out 81 81. Stauf didn't seem too happy about my victory, but I sure was.

I continued with my search for a cork. Where could it be? This felt like looking for a needle in a haystack. I got down on my hands and

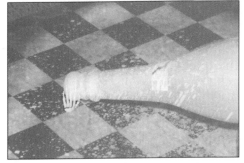

knees, trying not to inhale too much of the dust covering the carpet, and looked around in the dim light. Finally, on the floor to the left of the old television, I saw it! There was an unopened bottle of champagne, turned on its side on the floor.

As I took the cork out of the bottle, the GameBook came to life again, with a still image of Robin's smiling face. I swallowed hard at the sight of her, and pressed the play button.

"I'm researching a story on the Stauf Mansion," Robin said to the blonde waitress, who was sitting across the diner table from her. Way to go, Robin, I couldn't help thinking, so that's how you always bring back a great story, using that charm and persistence. I watched how the pretty waitress' face dropped at Robin's question. She's hiding something, Robin, I wanted to shout.

Robin continued as though she hadn't noticed the change in the other woman's expression. "You're the only person who's survived an encounter with the mansion."

I thought of that prosthetic hand, and shivered involuntarily.

I listened to the waitress'

response. "Who told you that?" She was trying to bluff it off.

"Everyone else has either disappeared or died." Good, Robin! Ignore the question, entirely.

The waitress looked uncomfortable. "It's all just stories," she said. And then the video ended.

What did these strange puzzles have to do with Robin? There seemed to be a strong connection between the ghoulish riddles posed by

the game book, the objects I found, and the video clips in the GameBook. Could it be that as I solved more puzzles, I would get to see more video pieces of what had happened to Robin?

Who was responsible for these videos and why were they being shown to me this way? Who'd sent me this GameBook in the first place? It was weird, but I had a feeling whoever did it was trying to be helpful, though I could have thought of some much direct ways to help.

And who was this waitress? What could she possibly have to hide, except that ghastly fake hand? I was beginning to get intrigued by the whole mystery, myself. For entire moments at a time, my fear faded, and I'd become totally absorbed by the puzzle of this house and the video clips I was seeing.

I closed the GameBook only to reopen it immediately, when it beeped again. I heard the smarmy voice of Henry Stauf tell me, *Artsy, excited lecher.*

The word artsy caught my eye. I recalled that there was an extensive portrait gallery in this house, although I couldn't exactly remember where it was. Stauf isn't so smart, after all, I thought, I'm starting to catch on to his stupid tricks. I wondered if there was another anagram hidden somewhere in this phrase. Artsy, excited lecher. Was there a portrait of a lecher somewhere in the Gallery?

I pressed the help key. Sure, when something's excited, it's all stirred up. Now I was confused, again. Stirred up?

Look for a lecher, read the next hint from my unknown ally. As if I hadn't figured that part out, already.

Artsy is an anagram of satyr. Of course! My eyes had already begun to rearrange the letters.

So there was a portrait of a satyr, was there? But where was the Gallery? I found it on the Map, but it was a disjointed room, all on its own. Defeated for the moment, I went back out to the hallway, the floor creaking as I went down the corridor. I descended the old staircase, trying to keep my little flashlight shining on each step before me.

As I walked around in the Foyer, feeling kind of helpless again, I noticed a small table to the left of the great staircase. It had a few chess pieces on it—another

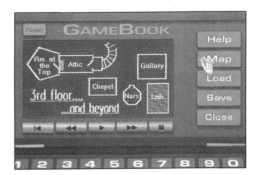

game. Some ripple of intuition told me that I'd need to play this one—
and win it—before I could find the secret of the Portrait Gallery. Secret
of the Gallery. . . was there a secret way to this secret location, perhaps?

I settled down to figure out the rules of this fragmented chess board.
The Gallery could wait for a moment. I'd get there next. As I peered
closer at the game, I saw that there were two knights of each color,
black and white. I'd played chess when I was a kid, so I knew
the moves of a knight, yet I was completely in the dark as to
what to do with these.

Consulting the GameBook seemed like the thing to do. I
ignored Stauf's sarcasm, and waited for that friendly female
voice to give me a hint. *Exchange the position of the white and
black knights using standard knight moves.* Well, that seemed
easy enough, though it would probably take some time. I wasn't sure
just how much of that I had to spare.

I pressed for more hints. *You can't move a knight off this odd section
of chessboard.* That restriction seemed to make the whole prospect
much trickier.

When the voice of my unknown friend said, *I think I could do it in 40
moves,* I realized that I had a genius on my side. Who was this woman,
anyway? I was starting to count on her help, and trusting that she would

be there, every time I got stuck. Well, I gritted my teeth. If she could do it in forty moves, then so could I!

It was just a matter of concentration, and I finally began to grasp what needed to be done.

Ultimately, I solved the little puzzle, and it might even have been fun, if the circumstances had been different. Stauf complained, "You got lucky that time." Poor loser.

I wasn't any closer to the Gallery, though. I started to poke around and, for some reason, I decided to take a closer look at the grandfather clock near the chessboard. As I examined this fine old antique, I opened

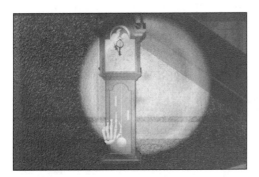
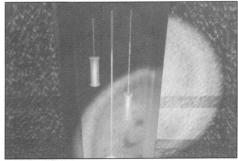

the bottom glass, wanting to take a look inside where the pendulum hung unmoving. I heard Stauf gasp, "Ooh, bad move!" but I ignored him and made a key discovery. This clock was more than it seemed at first glance. Inside was the entrance to a narrow secret passage.

This corridor was a kind of elongated crawlspace, though high enough that I could stand without stooping. It made sense to me that a haunted house would have secret passages! The condition of this particular secret passage, though, left a lot to be desired. In fact, it was barely even framed, as though thrown up in a hurry and left unfinished. Exposed 2x4s lined both sides of the walls, and there was a damp, sickly feeling around me. I thought I heard water dripping somewhere close by.

There was a ragged opening at the end of the passageway—and suddenly I was in the Portrait Gallery. I fancy myself an appreciator of art, and it was sad to see this room in such dilapidated condition; paint peeling off of the walls and empty spaces where other paintings had once hung. I imagined it must have been a beautiful place. Now it was just a shambles.

I noticed what looked like a Mondrian painting on the ground, propped up against the wall, beneath a painting of a girl in a blue dress.

As I came closer, it seemed to be another puzzle. I thought of messing with it right then, and have no doubt that I could have figured it out, but decided to pass on and tackle it later.

To the left of the small fireplace, there was a creepy-looking painting that was a mix of brown and gold tones. Underneath
the painting was a fallen statue of a woman's torso. It was a marble version of the Venus de Milo. I looked back at the creepy painting, which depicted the nude figure of a woman. As I got closer, I could see that she was struggling with—a satyr! Bingo! I touched the satyr

thoughtfully. What was Stauf trying to say? I didn't like the images this painting conjured up.

Then the GameBook popped open and I was watching a video sequence of two people I didn't know and had never seen before. The woman, whose name was Marie, was a seductive, smirky young thing. Dressed in a short, tight skirt and a white shirt that left little of her voluptuous shape to the imagination, she leaned in the doorway and vamped. She was asking for someone named Chuck. I guessed from the surroundings that this was the lobby of a cheesy motel.

The clerk, who obviously knew Marie, joked, "I thought you were here to see me."

She smiled long and slow, then sinuously leaned up against the counter, before replying, "You wish. . ." I watched as the hick behind the counter seemed momentarily unable to remove his gaze from her obvious attributes; their sheer endowment was proof of a kind and loving God. I noticed that my vision was stuck in the same place, too, and gave myself a shake.

Marie continued with a husky laugh, "Is he in his office?"

"He's got a meeting in five minutes. He hasn't got time for you today, Marie." The clerk waggled his head back and forth.

She smiled again. "Just tell him I'm here."

Whew. This girl was dangerous. She wore her sexual energy like a deadly weapon. Most of the women I knew were content with designer clothing. But who she was, and what, if anything, she had to do with Robin's disappearance, was still a total mystery to me. The video ended with the clerk picking up the desk phone.

As I wandered along the Gallery, looking at some of the faded paintings on the wall, the GameBook beeped me again. Bracing myself for another devilish jab from Henry Stauf, I opened it up to get the next clue.

A heart attack could put you into the ground. What in the world? I could feel my brain fogging over again, as I sought some kind of hidden meaning in the phrase.

Attack the word heart. Aha! heart was an anagram, wasn't it? I was really catching on, now! As I unscrambled the letters in an instant, I knew I was looking for earth. Earth. . . Of course! The globe! And that was in the Library.

I didn't even need the rest of the clues—*Another word for ground. Heart is an anagram of earth. I recall seeing a globe of the Earth.*

This was even starting to be kind of fun.

I had spent too much time resting on my laurels as a celebrity. My sleuthing skills, honed during years as an actual on-scene reporter, had long since atrophied. Now, slowly, I felt the return of old instincts and half-heard hunches.

It wasn't even that tricky for me to find my way out of the Portrait Gallery—the painting just to the left of the one depicting a man in a ten-gallon hat seemed to beckon to me, and I found it opened inward. I passed right through it and into the narrow passage that had led me here. Soon, I was back in the Foyer, squeezing my way out of the grandfather clock. For a moment, I thought I'd gotten mixed up and had

somehow not left the Gallery— I was standing in front of a crookedly hung painting of some birds in a tree.

Checking the Map, I noticed that all the areas were either blank or filled in except the Lab, which I had no idea how to find. I headed for the Library.

Gamer's Note:

Like the shortcut going up the stairs, here's a quick way to save a couple of steps by clicking on the stairs from just down the hallway. This will take you right to the bottom.

As I opened the door to the Library, a rising sense of anticipation churned my stomach. I was going to outwit all these puzzles and any other foolish thing that Stauf chose to throw at me! I reached down to the globe and gave it a spin.

Sure enough, the trusty GameBook responded with another video piece. Like pieces of a puzzle, I couldn't help thinking. As I watched, I saw a gorgeous pair of legs walk across a field, near a stream. They belonged to Robin, no doubt about that. I had a brief memory of happier times. She leaned down and touched a rock in the grass.

"Yeah, it's blood." A man's voice came from behind her, out of the camera's visual range. The video ended there, and I wanted to rip the little game machine apart. Was this the man who had made Robin disappear from the rest of the world? Would I get to find out who he was? I was frantic. Robin was in serious danger, I knew that. But I needed to know more.

Fortunately, the GameBook beeped me again, as soon as I took a step toward the door in the Library.

Stauf's maniacal voice chimed, *"BattleGround."*

BattleGround? It was too weird a word. It had to be an anagram. But for what? And why was the letter G capitalized?

Battle and ground are two words. The hint helped. Now I could tell that battle's letters, once rearranged, spelled tablet.

But what was the ground part all about? Something ground into bits? Not the ground we walk on.

The next hint, *Could ground be the past tense of grind?* seemed to uphold my idea that it was ground the verb, not ground the noun. But what did grinding have to do with a tablet?

Battle is an anagram. Battle is an anagram of tablet. No kidding, I thought. I'd already figured as much.

What was this supposed to mean? I realized I was in search of a tablet, but how or where I was to find it was beyond me. And what did the grind or ground part have to do with it? Was I looking for a whole tablet, or one that had been ground? Then it wasn't a writing tablet, was it? Unless my treasure-hunting object was a paper shredder, I doubted that conclusion. The only other tablet I could think of was a pill. You could grind a pill, no doubt. So, was I looking for a pile of aspirin dust?

Temporarily defeated, I sank down into the red armchair in the Library. It was plush and comfortable, and for a moment I had the image in my mind that its arms could come curling around me and trap me in the chair, holding me there, a prisoner of the Library forever. Man, I was really getting paranoid.

Was I licked? It sure felt like I had no options. Then I remembered. The only cross-hatched room left on the Map was the Lab.

It seemed reasonable to me that a tablet could be found in a laboratory. But how could I get there? Like the Gallery, the Lab was

marked as one of those rooms that had neither obvious entrance nor exit from any other room in the house.

I turned the information I already had over and over in my mind. What did I know? Where had I been? I ticked the places off on my hand. I'd been to the Library, the Foyer, the Gallery and

Dutton's Room. Dutton's Room. Wait a minute. In the bizarre account Robin had made me read about this house, there was something weird about Dutton's Room—but what was it?

I heard a creak behind me and nervously shifted my position in the chair. Why hadn't I paid closer attention to that book when I'd had the chance? What was its name again. . . something to do with the number seven? I couldn't remember.

But the vague details about Dutton's Room were swirling in my mind, like something I'd seen in a dream. I could almost get them to stay long enough to remember them, but not quite. Frustrated, I looked around the Library. Maybe something here would jog my memory. I looked around for several minutes, but nothing struck me as overly useful. The thought went through my mind—maybe I was just doomed to trial and error at every damned door in the house. I reached for the knob on the Library door.

And that's when I recalled the details of the book. Dutton's Room was unusual because of all the doors. It came to me in a flash, and I ran up the stairs, taking them two at a time. Dutton's closet door led to the Chapel. It was only through the Chapel that one could make it to the Lab!

Once in Dutton's Room, I went immediately through the closet door, the one to the left of the bed. Again I found myself in a narrow, dripping, damp passageway. I went down the uneven stairs carefully. I didn't want to trip and fall here. I came out of the passageway into the Chapel.

At the very rear of the Chapel, I found an arched doorway and

Gamer's Note:

Getting to Dutton's closet is tricky. One way is to watch the hand cursor and move it slowly toward the left edge of the screen, until it beckons. Click to go through the closet to the Chapel.

went through it. I was certain that this led to the Lab. When I saw the bloodied physician's table, I knew that I was in the right place. The sight of the blood made me queasy. I couldn't tell how fresh it was—didn't want to look that closely at it.

Searching around the Lab, I found what appeared to be an old medicine cabinet against a stone wall. There was a green lab bottle and other such accoutrements on the cabinet. Upon closer inspection, I found another devious puzzle on the cabinet, as well, contained in a little wooden box.

The wooden box had a mechanical windup key on its side. While I watched, a mechanical mouse came up from the bottom of the box, and sat on a platform in the center. Then the key wound itself, and all sorts of little wooden pieces appeared in the box, too, around the mouse. The pieces appeared to form a disjointed maze for the mouse. Like this crazy house is a maze for me, the thought came but I pushed it away. I had to win this game.

Stauf made some cheesy comment, but I was intent on getting some help from the GameBook. *Build a path for the mouse to find the orange hole.* I didn't exactly understand the specifics of that, but it seemed like a pretty simple thing to do. The first hint said I was playing against Stauf.

Placing a maze piece causes the other pieces in the row to slide over or a column to slide up and down. I could see that this was true. As a new piece came up to be played, if I put it at the end of a particular row, it would become the new end piece of that row. All the other ones would then shift over one place.

After a piece is played, you may move the mouse to any location along the newly created path. Even though I'd suspected all along that this was the case, having confirmation of it made my heart pound. It seemed as if it would just jump right out of my chest.

As I played, I learned that I was forbidden to put a piece at a row that Stauf had just played.

Finally, I found the way to build my path, bit by bit, and guided the mouse down the directions I wanted it to go.

Once I'd beaten Stauf at his own cat-and-mouse game, I noticed the green bottle next to the wooden maze. There was a pill on the cabinet, just in front of it. Without thinking twice, I snatched up the tablet.

And was rewarded with some of the most disgusting video footage I had yet seen. There was a head, bloodied and disfigured, among some rocks. As I watched in horror, the head faded into nothingness, leaving

the bloodied rocks behind as the only trace that it had ever been there. My forehead broke out in a cold sweat. I just wanted to leave this house.

Only the thought of Robin, trapped somewhere, no doubt by this fiend Stauf, kept me going. I turned to leave the Lab and was beeped again by the GameBook. Its cheery tone, although it had been annoying at first, was beginning to seem like my only friend. That was a real comforting thought. I was feeling more and more foolish for going along with this charade. I yelled a few obscenities at Stauf, who declined to answer. So I took up the GameBook again.

Bars deter cuckoo bird, chirped Stauf.

Doggedly, I searched the words for hidden meaning, spelling them backwards, forwards, looking for anagrams. As none came to mind, I clicked on the help button for a hint.

Maybe the cuckoo is not the bird! Great. So what was? Maybe I'm the cuckoo, I thought bitterly, maybe this whole thing is a wild goose chase and Robin is . . . I couldn't finish the thought.

Cuckoo means crazy. Well, whaddya know! By thinking myself nutso to be on this search, I was on the right track to solve this puzzle!

Bars deter is a crazy version of redbreast. Robin! Was that it? Would I find Robin now? But there were no more hints to be had.

Dejected, I turned, intending to return to the Chapel. But I got confused and ended up opening a strange arched doorway full of levers and gears. The door opened when I twisted the mechanism and I found myself in a dark tunnel. The tunnel led down into a vile, choking swamp that looked to have been a mausoleum or crypt. It was now full of some ghastly, glowing green muck that I avoided at all costs. I could not avoid the stench and the noxious fumes that rose from the unholy

stuff, and was coughing and gagging uncontrollaby by the time I escaped the crypt. My path took me into a basement passage, thankfully with clean dirt for the floor. Stumbling through an opening that seemed promising, I found myself in a strange room with three doors. I think my journey through the bowels of the mansion—for that was what it must have been—had unhinged me, and I rushed through the first door I came to, the one on the right. I found myself back in the hallway on the second floor. Checking the Map, I realized that I had just come out of Temple's Room. It took me several minutes to clear my head and regain my composure. Then I began again to gnaw on the puzzle Stauf had set before me.

I kept thinking that perhaps I'd missed something, that perhaps there was a photo of Robin somewhere, or a picture I'd overlooked, or something. I was on my way to the Gallery again, through the grandfather clock, when I stopped dead in my tracks. On the wall across from the clock, was that obnoxiously crooked, tacky picture of some birds in a tree. I'd noticed it when I came out of the Portrait Gallery, but had resisted the urge to straighten it.

The hair on the back of my neck stood up. I knew that this picture was significant. I didn't see why at first, since it was just a tree and some lousy birds. I stood, and studied the painting, didn't see anything.

Then it hit me like a hammer: The bird in the bottom right corner was a robin! Once I realized that, I touched it softly.

And that's when the time warp happened! That's the only way I can describe it. The painting faded away, although the frame remained, and there, behind it, surrounded by some surreal-looking pillars, was Robin herself! She was sitting on a staircase of some sort, and she was crying. Her blouse was ripped, and I wondered what had happened to her. I feared the worst.

It took me a long moment to realize that Robin was in the very crypt I had just, however unwillingly, visited. What was she doing there? Why had I not seen her?

"Oh god, help me. . . please help me." Was she crying?

Then the GameBook beeped, and as I looked down, I could see her in the screen—and a huge, Loch Ness-monsterish limb (was it arm or leg? how could I have known?) was coming up at her, right out of the bracken below the stairs! I shouted, "Robin, move! Get up! Look out!"

She looked around, as though she heard my voice. "Carl?" She asked of the air. But she moved, all right. And just in time, too, for that thing would have gotten her. I was anguished. Where was she? What happened next?

"Damn," I swore, as the GameBook went dead again. But at least Robin was okay for the moment. Where was she?

As I backed away from the painting, the GameBook beeped at me again. I opened it again, hoping for some clue that would tell me what was happening to Robin.

Modern art flourishes under the sun was all I got. Somehow I had the premonition that now was the time to return to the Gallery and play out that puzzle I had noticed before.

Is there any sun in this house? I had to laugh without feeling like laughing. If there was any sun in this house of horrors, I had yet to see it.

Flourish is to flower. Sunflowers, right? I was getting this.

I didn't need the last clue to know what to do. *Art under a sunflower.* I was already off to the secret passage in the grandfather clock that led to the Gallery.

Sure enough, the Mondrian was propped against the grimy wall underneath the painting of the girl in the blue dress, just as I'd recalled. What I'd neglected to notice is that the girl stood next to a giant sunflower!

As I looked closer, I noticed that the painting was all speckled and spattered with age, or as if something had been spilled upon it. It was an abstract painting made up of a lot of generally rectangular shapes. I noticed, too, that a shape became strangely illuminated if I touched it, and that other shapes in direct contact with the one I had chosen also became 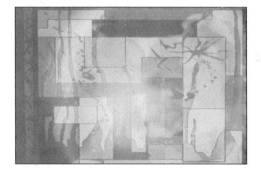 illuminated. When Stauf touched a shape, that shape and the ones touching it all turned grey.

The object is to choose the last possible space. It didn't take me long to see the strategy.

You can't choose a space that is adjacent to a previously chosen space.

I eventually figured out that there were some sections that were clear losers, but eventually, I found one section to touch for my first move, and from there it was easy. As usual, Stauf was none too happy that I had beaten him again.

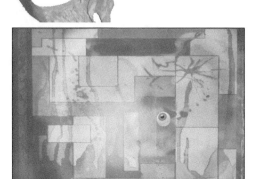

I saw the GameBook screen, with a still of Robin in the diner. Impatiently, I thought, I've seen this already. Is there some glitch? But then she was in her Mercedes, driving into town. I realized that I'd only seen bits and pieces of this video. Perhaps now some of the gaps would be filled in! I sat right down on the floor of the Gallery, leaned my back against the wall and prepared to grasp the whole chain of events.

My heart ached as Robin, graceful and beautiful as ever, slid out of the car, her briefcase in her hand, and went into the diner. Her business suit, black and sleek and appropriate to a New York City office, looked completely out of place in this small-town greasy spoon.

I had to chuckle when she asked for Perrier. The cook, Slim, seemed like a stereotype of every big, burly diner cook I'd ever seen in a TV sit-com. When he retorted, "Fresh out of Perrier, Eileen!" to the waitress, I couldn't help grinning.

The exchange between Eileen the waitress and Robin was unsettling. At first, it seemed all light and easy—in fact, I was straining to hear what Robin would say about me. ' "A man" ', huh? Well, you could sure say that again!

Then the conversation turned serious. Part of it I'd already seen, in the short clip before, with Robin asking about the house. Eileen's prosthesis was obvious, and when Robin mentioned the story about a dog, I shook my head. No dog ever did that. Was it the house? Had this place done that to Eileen? The idea was chilling.

Without wanting to, I looked around me to make sure no one was in the room with me, lurking in the shadows or oozing out of the paintings.

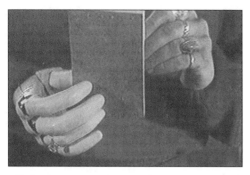

All the eyes in the paintings seemed to be watching me. It seemed safer to watch the video clips.

After the diner conversation ended, I saw that good-looking girl again, Marie, saunter into the Harley Motel. Although I'll admit I enjoyed watching her move, I was totally lost as to what her connection was with Robin, or anything else, for that matter.

That is, I was lost, until the desk clerk said into the phone, "Marie Wiley's here. . ." Marie Wiley. Not surprising, I reasoned, that in a small town lots of people would have the same surname. But Wiley was the same last name as Eileen's, the diner waitress, the only person to have survived an encounter with the Stauf Mansion! Surely that was more than just a coincidence! Perhaps they were sisters? Maybe Marie had been at the house as well? Maybe she knew the truth?

The scene changed into a tryst between Marie and her lover, Chuck, who obviously held some rinky-dink management job at the motel. She

managed to seduce him into missing a business meeting. I chuckled bitterly to myself. How many times had that nearly occured between Robin and me?

But this Marie girl was really twisted, I found. Out of spite, I guess, she bit the hell out of Chuck's neck, leaving a really obvious mark. Poor guy, he'd have

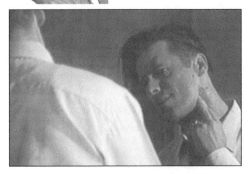

to go home to his wife and explain about how some wild animal had attacked him—not that that story wouldn't have been true enough! Marie was sexy enough to keep any man awake all night, but there was something wild and unpredictable about her, something in her personality that was a little too mischievous for my taste. It was mischief bordering on vindictiveness. While I speculated as to why she was like that, the scene switched again.

Robin was back walking through that field, discovering the blood on the rocks. I tensed up, remembering that unidentified male voice I had

heard in the previous clip of this scene—was it Stauf? As it turned out, it was only the police chief, a hickified local gun who doubtless had nothing better to do than chase beautiful women around his sleepy town.

Nice enough to warn her about the murders, though. Just what Robin needs to watch out for her, I thought, some folksy, cheeseball chief of police. I didn't like the way he looked at her, at all. He was just a bit too much on the friendly side. Damn him, he made Robin laugh, too!

After they walked away, that ghoulish head appeared between the rocks, then faded away. Was the whole area haunted, then?

Finally, I was looking at the piece I'd just seen, of Robin in

some damp cellar, with—hey, that was me! I was calling to her to move as that slimy claw came after her! How was it possible that I was being not only watched but videotaped as I moved around this house? Not for the first time, I wondered where these images were coming from. Were they sent by ghosts in the machine? I didn't see any cameras, anywhere. And what had become of Robin? This whole situation scared me all the way to my bones.

All I could do was push on ahead, trying to get closer to the truth of the house—and Robin.

My right leg had fallen asleep, and I was completely unaware of it until I stood up to leave the Gallery. I wobbled on my feet for a second or two, feeling the pins and needles rush into my leg. Suddenly, I heard the bonging of the grandfather clock—it chimed eight o'clock and I realized that I'd better hurry along. There was a lot to do, and I didn't relish the idea of being in a haunted house around midnight. Especially not Henry Stauf's house of horrors!

CHAPTER THREE

Eight O'Clock

As though it were answering a cue, the GameBook beeped. There was another clue waiting for me.

SkedAddled, proclaimed the voice of Henry Stauf. I wondered irritably, why won't he show himself? I was really getting tired of dealing with disembodied voices and video scenes of people I couldn't talk to.

SkedAddled, huh? I could tell from looking at the two words jammed together that sked must be an anagram. Of course. Desk! Where had I seen a desk? Could it have been in the Library?

The clues that followed weren't all that helpful, but I ran through them anyway, just in case. *This is two words again.* I'd already reached that conclusion, and gone two steps further.

Addled means all mixed up. Like I'd been earlier. But now I had a handle on things around here.

Sked is an anagram of desk. I was on my way to the Library, running across the Foyer.

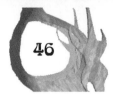

Once in the Library, I ran right over to the desk and looked at it. Hmm. There was an inkwell and an old pen on it, as well as a piece of paper. Did I want one of these? I leaned my hand on the desk, to the left of the inkwell, while I considered. I must have hit some hidden switch or something, because all the drawers opened and closed on the desk! Startled, I jumped back.

That's when the GameBook beeped me again, so I knew I'd done whatever needed to be done around the desk. I opened the GameBook, ready for my next clue.

Part of the body examined in the doctor's office. Well, I'd seen (but not looked too closely at) a heart in the Lab. Was that it? I frowned. No, you don't "examine" a heart in the doctor's office, you listen to one. So there had to be more to these words, again, than seemed obvious on the surface.

It must be another name for a body. This made no sense to me, but I was willing to go along with it. *Another name for body? A corpse?* Oh, God, no, I thought, not Robin! I tasted panic in my mouth, but calmed down, reminding myself that so far none of these clues had led to anything so grotesque.

Examine the body of the sentence. It's hidden in the words "doctor's office". Huh? I looked, and looked. Then I looked some more—and

found it! Torso! The last syllable of "doctor's", "T-O-R-S," along with the "O" in office!

Torso? I'd seen the marbled statue, the fallen one, in the Gallery. It would certainly count as a torso, I thought. I sighed. Back to the grandfather clock.

Before I headed into that dank passageway, I checked the Map to

see if anything had changed. I noticed that three new rooms now displayed the hatchmarks—Ba (I figured this was the Bathroom because of its size), Ed. Knox, and Game Room. But I was off to the Portrait Gallery for the moment.

In the Gallery, I went straight over to the fallen woman's torso on the floor, and touched the cold marble. The GameBook flashed another video on the screen.

It was Robin, walking into a cluttered doctor's office. She went up to the reception desk, and the girl behind the desk was none other than Marie Wiley! Surprise! Could have knocked me over with a feather. Gets around, doesn't she? It seems like she's got her finger in every kind of pie in Harley-on-Hudson. My curiosity about her was growing. What did she have to do with all this?

Marie looked pretty bored, and even annoyed. "Can I help you?"

Polite as always, Robin seemed to ignore the younger woman's rudeness, and asked to see Dr. Thornton. Of course. He was the doctor who'd treated Eileen Wiley all that time ago. It struck me as funny-peculiar that Marie, who was somehow related to Eileen, worked in his office.

"He's available. You a patient of his?" Marie was downright surly. Maybe she'd gotten up on the wrong side of Chuck's bed today.

While Marie tried to thrust a clipboard and forms at Robin, Robin explained, "Actually, I'm not here as a patient. I'm a producer for *Case Unsolved*—the television show?—and I'd like to interview him."

And then the segment of video was over. Burning with curiosity, I closed the GameBook, only to be beeped again by the next clue.

Libation for an affectionate puppy called Sounder. Was it whisky? Dogs had whiskers. I pressed the help key.

Sounder might be a key clue. So it was a homophone of some kind? A word that sounds like another . . . *What does an affectionate puppy do?* Huh? I hadn't had a puppy in so long I had to think about this one. Well, they squirm, they wag their tails, they drool, they snort, they sniff crotches, they lick unwilling victims. Where was the play on words in any of those?

A drink could be alcoholic. No, really?

Liquor and lick 'er sound alike. Aha! So I hadn't been that far off with my silly whisky thought! Liquor, huh? How 'bout that bottle of champagne in Brian Dutton's Room?

I went back up and found the fallen champagne cooler again. As I touched the bottle, I noticed that the cork I had taken out of the bottle had been replaced! How? I didn't want to know! As I touched the bottle, the cork popped out, seemingly on its own. I got to my feet, and the GameBook beeped at me, ready to give me another clue.

 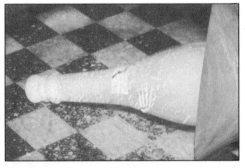

Animal sullied street. For some reason, I guess because of Eileen Wiley's hand and the puppy clue before, I immediately thought of a dog.

Sullied means messed up, the next hint said. That means one of the words is messed up—another anagram, I knew.

It's the street that's messed up. I looked carefully at animal, didn't see much. Street, though, rearranged itself in my mind to 'setter'.

Street is an anagram of setter. So my instincts had been right, about a dog! But where was I going to find a setter? When in doubt, I thought, consult the Map.

There was nothing to find on the 1st Floor; the Library and the Foyer showed up as solid blue. No other rooms indicated that I had anything to do in them—yet. On the 2nd Floor, however, there were the three possibilities I had noticed earlier. I ruled out the Bathroom as a likely place to find a setter. Edward Knox's Room was a likely place, and so was the Game Room, I reasoned.

I was still in Brian Dutton's Room. I would head down the hall, investigate the Game Room, and then look in Edward Knox's Room if I'd yet to find a setter.

I went all the way down the hall, passing the still-life painting for what seemed like the hundredth time, and the strange lion statue on the floor caught my eye as I went by.

The Game Room seemed darker than many of the rooms I'd seen. Or maybe I was just paranoid. There was an enormous pool table in the middle of the floor, with an old tiffany lamp hanging above it. The balls on the table were in perfect formation, though not for the start of a billiards game, I noticed. As I looked closer, I realized that they formed another puzzle for me to solve.

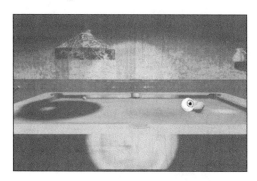 

There were nine balls, all cue balls, on the table, arranged in three diagonal rows. All together, the balls formed a diamond shape on the faded green felt.

"You're behind the eight ball, and don't even know it," quipped Stauf. What was the point of this puzzle? I consulted the GameBook for some help.

"Don't listen to him, Carl. You're doing fine!" said the female voice, in reassuring tones. Who was my unseen supporter? She had

great courage, to oppose a force like Henry Stauf. Would I ever get to meet her? Was she even—I gulped at this thought—human?

Replace all of the nine white balls with the numbered balls in sequential order. I had no idea what this meant. But I'd figure it out.

There are hidden lines of influence between the balls. Figure out what they are and you can solve this mystery. So, in some way, this was consistent with the science of pool playing. Well, I'd shot some pool in my day, and was no stranger to the game.

I noticed if I touched a ball, it would turn into the number one ball. If I touched the same ball, again, the number would fade. Okay, so I could undo any mistakes I made. When I touched another ball, having already made the number one, it would turn into the number two. Now I understood! My job was to get all of the balls changed to numbers, in order.

I played around with the balls, changing the numbers and getting stuck, until I found the right combination of initial moves. From then on, it was pretty simple, and I went on to solve the puzzle, putting all nine balls in place. Stauf responded cordially, but coldly, to my success.

Now that all the balls were in order, I looked around the room. Were there any setters here?

I suppressed a grim laugh when I saw the painting of the dogs playing poker on the wall, near the chess table. It seemed like such a . . . well, a normal sight. Really out of place in this creepy mansion. Reaching out my hand to the setter, I gave him a little pat.

The GameBook came back on, and I was looking at the face of the older man I assumed was Dr. Thornton.

Robin asked him, "But really, doctor, what did it look like to you?" in her best, no-nonsense-but-smoothly-caring investigative voice.

He paused for a moment before answering sadly, "Robin, it was a mess. A bloody mess."

Geez, thanks for warning me, doc. I watched the screen, rooted in horror. There was a young woman in an orange shirt and short skirt, writhing on the doctor's examining table. A much younger Doctor Thornton was next to her, apparently trying to hold her down, or comfort her, or I couldn't tell what. There was blood on his hand.

The young woman was screaming, and screaming, and screaming. The animal-like sound of her abject pain seemed to go right through my body. I got a shiver up my spine, and every hair on my body stood on end. Then I actually saw the source of the

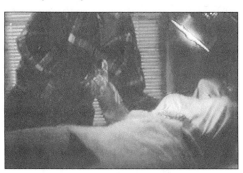 young woman's pain. Her right arm came up off of the examining table—and I saw the bloody stump that had been Eileen Wiley's hand. Tendons and all. It was a ghastly sight, and my own wrist began to ache as I imagined the pain she must have been suffering in that moment.

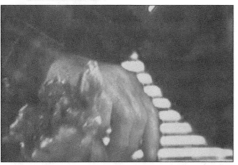

I gagged in complete revulsion and sank down to the floor of the Game Room, lightheaded and stomach churning. Closing the GameBook, I leaned over to put my head in between my knees, and waited for the nausea to pass.

Once I'd steadied myself and could swallow again without feeling a burning lump in my throat, I sat upright on the Game Room floor and propped my back against the wall. No dog did that. The words went around in my mind, over and over again like some demented meditation mantra. No dog could have done that. Eileen's hand had been severed, at the wrist. I could see again that pitiful bleeding stump in my mind, like some videotape that wouldn't shut off, and hear the echo of her screams. No doubt they would provide the soundtrack of my nightmares for a long time to come.

I didn't want to think about it anymore. Something other than a dog had deprived Eileen Wiley of her right hand, and although I wanted to know what had done so, I was in no hurry to encounter the same force. I wanted to leave this house with both of my hands, and every other part of me, intact.

And what about Robin? a voice in my head asked. Surely nothing will happen to her. After all, I was here to find her and get her out of here, wasn't I? Yup, that's me. Carl Denning, knight in shining armor.

I stood up, and hadn't taken two steps through the Game Room when the GameBook beeped me. I opened it up, as I thought, to hear another clue. I was greeted instead by silence.

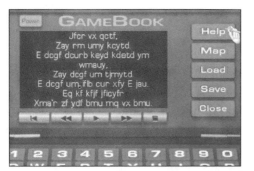

As I glanced at the screen, I thought at first that the GameBook was malfunctioning. There was gibberish scrawled across the screen. Oh, God, no, I pleaded to my invisible helper, don't you leave me in here with no help at all! But then I calmed down, realizing that the gibberish letters were organized into small groups that could pass for words. So it was encoded in some way.

The first hint from my female friend supported this theory. It definitely looks like an encrypted message. I needed more than that.

Xma'r translates to "You'd." I didn't want to ask how she knew that. I just wanted to solve the thing.

The son of a son is a grandson. And he'd be a grandfather. I'd be sure to keep that in mind.

No watch. Did this have anything to do with the clock?

A clock has hands and face. Yup, it's the grandfather clock, isn't it? But I had to be sure. I needed to decode the message.

Clearly I was going to have to write this down. I took the coded message, wrote it out on a piece of paper, and wrote the word "you'd" under "xma'r." Then I filled in under each "X," the letter "Y." And under every "M," the letter "O," under each "A" the letter "U," and under each "R" the letter "D." So it looked like this:

Jfcr vx qctf, Zay rm umy kcytd. E
  d   y   u   do   o

dcgf dcurb keyd kdetd ym wmauy,
       d   o   o

Zay dcgf um tjmytd.
u   o   o

E dcgf um iflb cur xfy E jau.
    o   d y   u

Eq kf kfjf jficyfr
           d

Xma'r zf ydf bmu mq vx bmu.
you d   o   o   y   o

Once that was done, I could kind of see how words might be formed in there. "vx . . ." I didn't know many two-letter words that ended with a "Y." My, by. . . and that was it! So "vx" was either "my" or "by." And then, that hint about the son of a son. I figured that those words must be located somewhere in the mixed up text. The last four words had plenty of "O's" in the right places for son. Perhaps it's "son of my son," I mused. Then "vx" would indeed be "my." I tried it that way, filling in the letters I knew, now. I felt that I was on to something.

Jfcr vx qctf, Zay rm umy kcytd. E
  d my f   u   do   o

```
d c g f   d c u r b   k e y d   k d e t d   y m   w m a u y ,
           n d s                               o       o n

Z a y   d c g f   u m   t j m y t d .
  u               n o       o

E   d c g f   u m   i f l b   c u r   x f y   E   j a u .
              n o             n d  y           u n

E q   k f   k f j f   j f i c y f r
  f                   d

X m a ' r   z f   y d f   b m u   m q   v x   b m u .
y o u  d                s o n   o f   m y   s o n
```

"A" was "C," I was pretty sure. The word "cur" had "_nd" under it. It could only be the word "and!" My next guess was that "E" was "I"—not only was it capitalized and stood alone, but the 'a' was already taken, and no other letter stood alone as a word. As I filled in these letters, it also became apparent to me that the third word must be "face," like the clue. So "F's" were "E's"! I'd have this done in a jiffy, now.

```
J f c r   v x   q c t f ,   Z a y   r m   u m y   k c y t d .   E
  e a d   m y   f a c e      u       d o  n o        a  c        I

d c g f   d c u r b   k e y d   k d e t d   y m   w m a u y ,
 a  e      a n d s     i           i c       o       o u n

Z a y   d c g f   u m   t j m y t d .
  u       a e n o   c     o   c

E   d c g f   u m   i f l b   c u r   x f y   E   j a u .
I    a e n o    e             n d  y e        I   u n

E q   k f   k f j f   j f i c y f r
I f    e     e   e     e a    ed

X m a ' r   z f   y d f   b m u   m q   v x   b m u .
y o u  d     e     e  s o n   o f   m y   s o n
```

And, finally, it all made sense.

> *Read my face, but do not watch.*
> *I have hands with which to count, but have no crotch.*
> *I have no legs and yet I run.*
> *If we were related, you'd be the son of my son.*

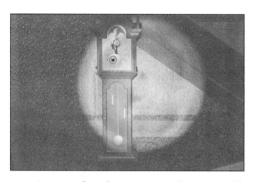

Certainly, this meant the grandfather clock, and I was off down the stairs in such a reckless hurry that I didn't even bother to look where I put my feet. Back in the Foyer, I stood in front of the clock and examined its face. I reached out to touch the hands, and was gently rocked side to side, as though I'd become part of the pendulum for a moment. It was an eerie and uncomfortable feeling, to be a part of that clock.

I was on my way back to the staircase when I was thoroughly startled by the unexpected presence of a woman. How had she come in without my hearing? And then I realized with a start that this was no ordinary girl. For one thing, I could see right through her! She was a ghost!

I wanted to run away, but my feet wouldn't move at all. Then she spoke to me, and I felt my fear melt away. She was a teenager, this ghost, and a scared one at that. We have our fear in common, I thought. Although I was stunned, I stood where I was. She was young, and blonde, and wanted me to help someone named Samantha.

"Something's got her," she explained in a trembling voice.

Samantha? I didn't know any Samantha. "I . . .uh . . Who's Samantha?" The question sounded lame and awkward to me, but it was the only thing I could think of to say. How did one help ghosts, anyway?

"Can you help her?" pleaded the girl, tearfully, looking at me but looking through me at the same time. I felt the hair on my back standing up. Something in her voice seemed familiar. I searched her face. I'd seen this face before. But where?

I answered tentatively, wanting to keep talking to the ghostly teenager until I could figure out who she was. "I . . . I don't know."

She looked as though she were about to crumble beneath her fear and grief. "I have to get out of here . . . I'm scared!"

With that, she turned and ran away, off into the mists of the darkened house and some other time and dimension. I stretched out my hand, trying to bring the ghostly girl back. "Wait . . ." I shouted into the thin air. Maybe she could still hear me. "Where's Robin?"

But she was gone. It seemed to me that the house was laughing at me, mocking my frustration. "Damn!" I exclaimed, furious and helpless.

I turned it over in my mind. Obviously, this girl had been in the house at some other time. This was a replay of some event that had happened before. . . her familiarity bothered me. Why couldn't I place her? She was blonde. The only other blonde I'd seen, through the videos. . . of course! It was Eileen Wiley. Not the Eileen I'd seen as a tough-talking, quick-witted diner waitress, but a younger, defenseless Eileen, with her right hand intact. The ghost had worn the face of fear. She'd begged for my help—for someone named Samantha. "Something's got her," I heard her voice in my head.

Something in the house? I wanted to shout the question out loud, but was afraid of the answer I'd get. Frankly, I didn't want to ponder any more bizarre questions. I wanted my mind to be quiet and stop badgering me with what I didn't understand. Had Eileen come to the house with another girl, then? Samantha? Why had I heard nothing of this—had Samantha been . . . had she disappeared, too?

And where was Robin?

The only answer to these questions was a faint breeze in the Foyer, as though the house found my futility somehow amusing.

Just then, before I really went crazy and succumbed to my urge to yell at the mansion, the GameBook beeped again.

More gibberish, this time read by a mocking Stauf. I swallowed hard, and got down to work. First things first. I pressed the help key.

It's another encrypted message. A type-righter might help solve this one. Type-righter? I didn't exactly follow.

It's as if the letter of a keyboard were shifted to the right. Ohhh, now I got it. Using the GameBook's keyboard, I was able to substitute the letters. The "Z" and "A," at the left end of their rows, simply became the letters at the opposite end of their respective rows. "Z," then, became "M." "A" became "L." It was really quite easy.

Zu gotdy od mpy nrmy stpimf.
My first is not bent around

Zu drvpmf zrsmd
My second means

Aogy jrt iq
Lift her up

Pt
or

Viy jrt yp yjr htpimf.
cut her to the ground

Something not bent is—what? Straight, obviously.

Lift her up is to raise her. Raise her. My first—word, right?—was straight. My second, raise her. *Cut her to the ground? Raze her?* Razor! Straight razor.

The logical place for a razor was in the Bathroom. I was off, headed up the stairs, again. They creaked, as always. The sound was almost reassuring. At least I still existed in the real world; I wasn't a ghost yet.

As I pushed open the squeaky door into the Bathroom, I got a distinct whiff of a humid, musty odor, as though someone had just taken

a shower in here—in swamp water. Revolted, I understood that moist, cloying feeling as soon as I walked in the door. The tub was full, all right, but not with water. It was filled to the brim with blood! A half-immersed skeleton lay in it, the skull smiling up at me in a frozen and ghastly expression. Or perhaps I only imagined that's what I saw.

There was blood all over the base of the sink, and it had spattered onto the tiles of the floor, as well. I felt that nausea rising again in my stomach, and turned away.

Over on the floor, to the right of the tub, was a drain. It seemed that a lot of the blood from the floor was going there—I moved closer to get a better look at that strange drain. There was a peculiar-looking spider's web over it.

I knew this was yet another devious puzzle. But what was I supposed to do?

Swap the positions of the brown spiders on the top with those of the white spiders on the bottom.

You can move along straight lines only from one point to the next.

It must be done in seven moves.

A move is complete when another spider is selected.

Well, that last clue was helpful in the end. I was able to switch the spiders' positions in seven moves according to the rules, but in reality, I moved 16 times. And I solved the puzzle.

The razor was on the edge of the bathtub. I gingerly reached out a finger to tap it. It opened on its own, then closed, and for some reason, I had an image of my finger stuck in its sharp embrace. Then the GameBook screen glowed with the interesting image of Marie kissing her hotel manager, Chuck.

This is gonna be a good one. Despite Robin's disappearance and visits from ghosts and Eileen's missing hand and the strain of being in

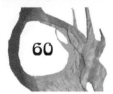

this haunted mansion, I still had a cynical sense of humor. I figured anything Marie was up to was probably no good—but she sure was sexy and fun to watch.

Marie and Chuck were kissing passionately, teeth exposed and tongues slithering around. All of a sudden, with no warning at all, she held a straight razor to his throat. Chuck tensed, his eyes moving slowly down to look at Marie. I gasped out loud. I knew she was dangerous, but this was beyond extremes.

The video faded and I found myself wondering whether little Marie had actually sliced his throat open. Somehow, I wouldn't have put it past her.

As I was beeped again by the GameBook, I didn't have too much time to contemplate Marie and her pathetic games.

It was time to return to Stauf and the sick odyssey he had me on.

Fruit Loop on stove. Was it an anagram? I looked carefully at both words, but loop making either pool or polo didn't seem like likely leads.

A loop is shaped like an "O". So was I looking for a round fruit? Ruled out pears, bananas and avocadoes right off the bat. This was going to be tricky, I could tell.

Is there another word for stove?

Oven? Range? I was just guessing wildly.

Wait a minute. Range. O + range. . . hmmm. I pressed the Help key again. *"O" plus "RANGE" spells orange.* Well, I consulted the Map. The Kitchen had nothing for me to do, so I thought maybe I'd find an orange in the Dining Room.

When I reached the stairs, I noticed an orange in the painting at the top, but when I tried to touch it, Stauf only taunted me. It was not the orange I was looking for. As I slid open the double doors to the Dining Room, I was struck by how cheery this room must once have been. The walls were done in a faded purplish paper, and there were attractive windows at the far end of the room. I imagined that many lively dinner conversations had taken place at this table, long ago. The table itself was a wreck, cluttered with broken crockery and some cobwebbed candlesticks. There was a peculiarly iced cake on one side of it that didn't look too appetizing—it appeared to be in the shape of an insect or something, a giant cockroach maybe. Perhaps it was another puzzle, but I really didn't care to get close enough to find out.

This was all fine and dandy, but there didn't seem to be any oranges around, and if there were, I imagined I'd find nothing more than a pile of mold and rot. I took a few steps around the room, just to make sure I was wasn't missing something. There was a cabinet, a few chairs, and a couple of paintings.

Aha! I was after one of the paintings—another still life—this time of a bowl of fruit! As I ran my hand over the orange, a giant worm emerged from the inside of the banana and ate another one, from inside the orange. I drew my hand back, disgusted. More of Stauf's repulsive humor. I blinked, and then the still life was, again, still.

I turned to get away from that slimy painting, before any more maggots appeared. The GameBook beeped me. I opened it with less

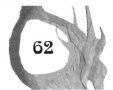

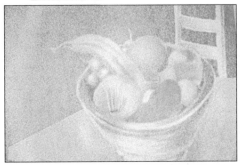

enthusiasm than before, waiting for the next demented task. Would this ordeal ever end? Where was Robin? And when would I find her?

Looking back, I realize that I must have been under some sort of spell. I mean, in the cold light of day, it seems absurd to have continued playing along with this madman. Yet something told me that if I didn't play along, he would do something horrible to Robin—if he hadn't already! And I, too, was a prisoner in this evil house. I was all too aware that my own safety was not assured. I continued to play along.

Dreams abound of arming the rebels. What of nocturnal horses schedules? I read it over again, once or twice, and then laughed out loud. That was an easy one, Stauf old boy, I thought, you must be slipping. I could see nightmares written all over the statement.

In the off-chance that I was confused, I flipped through the hints, anyway. *Rebels could be rebels.* Fine, I nodded. We'd been through some noun-for-verb susbstitutions already.

"Arming the" rebels. It's an anagram! I saw the word 'nightmare' in it.

There's a painting of Fuselli's "Nightmare" somewhere in this house. I consulted the Map. I could tell that Ed Knox' Room was my destination. As I made a left at the top of the stairs, it was the first door on the right.

The faded Confederate flag was the first sight that met my eyes in Ed Knox' Room. I didn't think that was the nightmare I was in search of.

On the other side of the room, there was an old mirror. Parts of its surface had peeled away or were tarnished or something. It presented a really disturbing, patchy appearance. I went to take a closer look, and noticed it was really another psychotic puzzle from Stauf. I'd have to solve it before I tried anything else in Knox' Room.

As I got closer to it, my vision seemed to twist and distort, until I was staring at the mirror turned on its side! It broke into several pieces, like one of those square, moving parts puzzles that form a picture, the kind that kids play.

I went to the GameBook, enduring another of Stauf's little attempts at humor. "Isn't this a pain," he said. Or was that "pane"?

By sliding the individual panes, restore the mirror to its original state. But what was its original state? Before it was half-rotted away? Or just the way I had seen the mirror before the puzzle began. I decided it was that last option.

Use the desilvering sections of the mirror as clues to the solution. Okay, I would.

It took some doing. I tried to keep a mental image of the mirror the way I had first seen it in my head. When I gave up and wanted to start over, I found that the panes had realigned themselves differently this time. After a while, though, I finally slid the last piece into place and was rewarded by another of Stauf's nasty comments. I was almost getting used to him—a scary thought in itself.

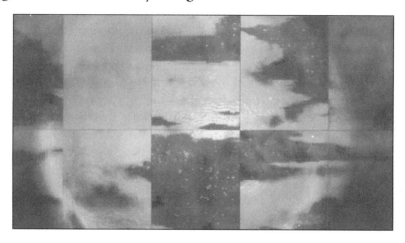

On the wall above the fireplace, there was a gruesome painting. It showed a woman, asleep, with a horned creature sitting on her chest, and a horse's face peering through the curtains. I deduced that it must be Fuselli's "Nightmare", and went over to touch it. I put my hand right over the horse's face, and wondered ironically if it really was a mare.

Then the video screen in the GameBook came up, and there was Robin, running along through some forest. She ran up the side of a wooden construction—was it a house, maybe a barn? I couldn't tell for sure—and ran right into that cheezy Chief of Harley Police. They both registered a moment of surprise, and then the clip was over.

I couldn't get it out of my mind that somehow this nightmare painting and Robin running into the Chief of Police were related. Was the Chief—Jim, he called himself—not entirely what he seemed? I was suspicious of everybody by now.

The insistent beeping from the GameBook woke me out of an unhappy trance about Robin and that uniformed Casanova. It was time for the next clue.

A distant, ancient Castle Keep
This famous Prince a place to sleep
To sleep, perchance to dream
Of an upset teagarden indochine.

This was really getting weird. To sleep, perchance to dream. I knew this was Shakepeare, and after some thought, remembered that it was from Hamlet. Well, he was a famous prince, after all.

The first clue was about as helpful as the rhyme itself. *It is Hamlet to which it refers, yet it is not Hamlet.* What the . . . ?

An upset teagarden is anagrammed. Well, that made sense. I couldn't figure out what a teagarden would be doing, in a verse about Hamlet otherwise. But what did the Indochine part mean?

And teagarden could be two words. Like tea and garden? Or did it anagram to two words?

Boy, did I ever feel silly, when the final hint came up. *Teagarden is an anagram of Great Dane.* Of course, Hamlet was a Danish king!

Hadn't I seen a painting with a dog in it, before the one in the Game Room? I had to think about that for a while. As I walked out of Knox' Room, and along the corridor, I realized again how weirdly obsessed I had become with beating this house at its own game.

I went slowly down the stairs, thinking about that dog painting. Abruptly, as if by instinct, I veered off to the left at the base of the stairs, and went into the Library. There it was! Behind the telescope! The Great Dane picture, much faded and dilapidated. I touched it, and

nothing special happened. I turned around in the Library, and was met by the second ghost I'd ever seen in my life.

He was an odd-looking man, in a smoking jacket with an ascot at his throat, holding a book by the Marquis de Sade. I recognized his face as the face of Brian Dutton. I'd seen it in an old photograph, in that book of Robin's about this place. "Ah," he said urbanely. "I didn't hear you come in—you gave me quite a fright." That was a laugh. I gave him a fright? Or was he even talking to me? I sincerely hoped not!

"Amazing thing, this," he continued. "Absolutely amazing the things the Marquis has come up with, don't you think?" This was so bizarre, I didn't know what to think.

He repeated, "Absolutely amazing."

Before I could respond, he had disappeared, book and all.

I'm sure my jaw was on my chest. It was going to fall a lot lower. Just then Marie faded into the room where Dutton had been standing, leading a huge dog on a leash. Was it really Marie, or just some ghostly form of her? I couldn't be sure and didn't want to get close enough to her to find out. Her hair was all pulled back, behind her head. She looked many times older than she was, and she was dressed in a black brassiere and some kind of black tights, with a spiked black collar around her throat. In the Village in New York I might not have given her a second glance, but here. . . Here, it was enough to make your head resemble a cactus, covered in spikes of hair that stood straight up in all directions!

She pulled the dog around in front of her, and yelled "Sit!" in a shrill voice that made me want to turn tail and run away yelping. I probably would have done so, too, if I'd have thought that I wouldn't have attracted her attention. As it was, I was so scared I didn't want to breathe.

"Good boy. Now speak!" she commanded the German shepherd. The dog whined for a moment, and then started to howl. As it howled, its face changed into the face of the clerk from the motel. His teeth were bared and his face was straining with the effort of his dog-like howl.

As for Marie, she stood there and laughed maniacally. The sight of her wide grin was so ghoulish and the grating sound of her laughter so macabre, my head was spinning from the horror of it all. I was so wrapped up in the possible meaning of the hotel clerk's face on the dog's body that I almost didn't notice her face changing. Oh, God, but change it did, into an evil, foul version of Marie. Before my disbelieving eyes, she sprouted giant fangs, the shape of her head twisted and distorted, and a great pointed tongue sprawled out of her mouth.

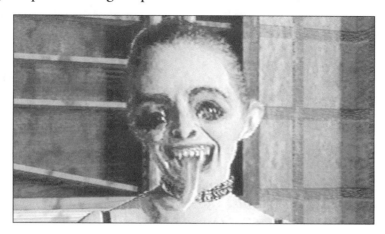

Suddenly the devilish vision was gone. Marie had vanished, the dog was howling no more, the Library was silent once again. I wiped the back of my hand across my brow, and was only vaguely aware that it came back damp from sweat.

I opened the GameBook. I had to get on with this, and get out of here as quickly as I could. And I decided, if I ever got out of here, to make it a point not to meet this Marie chick. She was real bad news.

A man-horse on the fly sounds like a wounded bull's eye. A man-horse? A centaur? Maybe a flying centaur? Were there any anagrams in here that I was missing?

The word "sounds" indicates a homophone. This wasn't helping me out too much. Or maybe I was just dense, still recovering from the shock of Marie turning into some kind of demon before my eyes.

A bull's eye is the center of the target. Cen + tar?

A man-horse is called a Centaur. I knew just where to find one. I'd seen a similar sculpture in the Chapel. Sort of a gryphon, but maybe it was a winged centaur . . .

I closed the GameBook with a snap, and quickly went from the Library, up the stairs to Dutton's Room. I went throught the door to the left of the Dutton's bed, and found myself once more in the Chapel.

There was an old, faded smell of incense hanging in the air. I went straight down the center aisle, and just to the left of the great door that led to the Lab, I found the stone sculpture I was looking for. Upon close scrutiny, it still looked more like a gryphon to me, but I sensed I was on the right track, anyway. As I knelt down to touch it, the curious triangle on its side caught my eye. Another crazy puzzle to get through!

It was a series of hexagons, all piled one on top of the other, forming the triangle which had originally gotten my attention. But what was I to do?

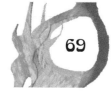

I noticed that if I put one of my red pieces on a hexagonal box, Stauf would promptly play a blue one. What did this mean?

Upon consulting the game book, I was told: *To win, be the first to create an unbroken path that touches all three sides of the triangular field.* So, the idea was to connect adjacent red pieces until my paths made two paths, one from side to side of the triangle, and one touching the base of it. I assumed that Stauf would try to block my efforts as he tried to make his blue paths touch all three sides.

A corner hexagon counts as touching two sides at once. This was the last hint I received about this game. I was on my own in my effort to defeat Stauf's little blue pieces.

 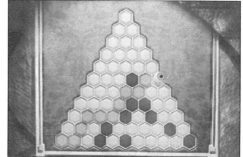

After trying it a few different ways, it became clear to me that the best and surest way to win was to begin from the middle, working my way over to one side. Once this strategy was clear to me, I had no problem connecting my red pieces and upsetting Stauf's attempts to prevent me from winning. I was ready to move on, but first I had some catching up to do in the world of videotape. I made myself comfortable in one of the Chapel pews, opened the GameBook and pressed Play.

There was an opening scene of the Police Chief and Robin, standing on a sidewalk somewhere. He drove up in his police jeep to the yellow house with a picket fence. Robin followed in her convertible. So he'd escorted her to Doc Thornton's—I wished chivalry were really dead. Judging from the amount of speaking glances they exchanged, a lot of sexual tension was brewing between Robin and the policeman.

Just like a woman, I thought savagely. I felt all of the hurt coming back, bleeding like a picked scab. I'd come all the way from Connecticut, gotten myself trapped in this horrible place, seen ghosts and felt nothing but fear and paranoia since I entered the Stauf Mansion. For what? Was Robin truly that fickle? I found that I didn't have an answer to that question.

Or was she just lonely and scared? Was it purely a chemical thing between them, her and "Jim"? Had she forgotten all about me? If he was her new interest, how come he wasn't here, saving her? Then I remembered that she'd called out for me, in desperation. I sighed deeply and went on watching the video. There was just a nagging question about what Robin really did on those frequent business trips. How many "Jims" were out there?

With a few backward glances at Jim, Robin walked into the doctor's, and for the second time I watched the scene between her and an openly hostile Marie Wiley.

When Robin mentioned Eileen Wiley and the house, the doctor seemed pretty reluctant to tell her anything.

"Lot of stories about that old house," he blustered, in his pleasant, down-home kind of way. He held on to the line that Eileen's hand had been bitten off by a dog. It didn't come as any real surprise to me that

he'd never before or since seen a hand bitten by a dog. Probably wasn't too shocking to Robin, either, though she diplomatically let that one ride.

"But really, doctor, what did it look like to you?" As soon as that question was out of her mouth, I shut my eyes. I didn't want to see Eileen Wiley's severed wrist again.

Once the pitiful screams had faded off, Robin said to the doctor, "I just think there's more to this Eileen Wiley thing than meets the eye."

The camera shifted, and there was Marie, using the intercom to eavesdrop on Robin's conversation with Doc Thornton! Marie didn't look too happy, either. Snoopy. I'd already decided that Marie was a twisted little bitch, but she also seemed to be involved in a lot of these videos. She must have something to do with Robin's disappearance. Didn't like the big-city producer snooping around. But why? What did she have to hide?

The doctor asked if Robin had managed to ask Eileen about the past and was even kindly in his demeanor when Robin explained that she hadn't gotten too far on the subject with Eileen. He reminded Robin that it had been a traumatic time for her, implying that it wasn't too suprising that she'd be unwilling to talk about it with a complete stranger.

I think Robin understood, and she probably felt a great deal of empathy for the diner waitress. But Robin was persistent, too—that was one of the things I'd liked best in her.

"It's just that she's the only one who's had an experience at the mansion and lived to tell about it."

The gentle doctor's response to this statement was a real jaw-dropper. "Not the only one." It was said clearly, as though it were an

undisputed fact. The fleeting thought crossed my mind that this man had gone totally senile, and was confusing one thing with another. I guessed that Robin had a similar reaction, for all of her surface politeness.

Any questions I had about his mental acuity were erased, though, when he named the other person who'd survived an encounter with this horrific mansion. "Samantha Ford."

". . . happened to Samantha. Something's got her." I heard it clearly in my mind, the voice of the young Eileen Wiley, the ghost I'd met in the Foyer. Samantha! But what had become of her?

The doc was telling about how Eileen and Samantha had sneaked into the Stauf Mansion. He expained that hardly anyone knew about the fact that Samantha had been there, too. Her family was influential and managed to hush the whole thing up.

His final word on the subject was a real show-stopper. I thought I was used to shocks by now, but Doctor Thornton proved me wrong on that. "But if you think Eileen's hand is a mystery, well. . ." he said with a certain dramatic emphasis, "Samantha has been paralyzed from the waist down and confined to a wheelchair ever since that night!"

I shuddered to think what might have befallen the mysterious Samantha.

Then the video changed, and I saw myself in the house, and re-experienced the conversation with the ghost of a young Eileen Wiley. So Samantha had been "gotten" by something in the house. I closed my eyes in horror at the thought.

When I opened them, I saw again that passionate kiss between Marie and Chuck, at the dam. She brandished the straight razor, and

I held my breath. As he looked down at her, she took it from his throat and slipped it into his jacket pocket with some kind of a knowing glance. Then I was looking at running water, and then there was silence.

The next part of the video showed Eileen in the diner, smoking a cigarette. It was dark outside, and it must have been closing time, as she was dressed in nicer clothes then her work uniform. For the first time,

she struck me as an attractive woman. Marie came in, for a cup of coffee and a smoke. She looked younger and more carefree than I'd seen her in some of the other videos, as if keeping up a facade for her mother.

Eileen looked troubled as she lit a cigarette for Marie, "You know I don't like you smokin', Marie." The level of tension between mother and daughter was pretty high.

As soon as Eileen mentioned Chuck Lynch, Marie's face shut down and she got all sullen.

Eileen remonstrated, "He's a married man." It was obvious that her concern for her daughter was sincere, and that her primary reason for saying anything had to do with Marie's reputation. "I don't want people calling my daughter a tramp."

Oh, brother, Eileen, I thought, if you only knew that's the least of your daughter's problems!

"Yeah, well, like I said .. like mother like daughter." With that sneer, Marie was off her seat in a huff and headed for the door.

Eileen Wiley looked helpless and even bewildered in the face of her rebellious and belligerent daughter. I felt really sorry for her as she called out "Marie!" in a shocked voice, trying to sound parental but coming off as shrill and ineffective. Marie spun around, the hate in her eyes so potent even I felt it.

"What?" she spat out at her mother.

The older woman seemed to wilt. It was a battle of wills, and Eileen was clearly on the losing side. "I . . . uh . . will you be home tonight?" she asked plaintively.

Marie's provocative grin stretched from ear to ear. She knew perfectly well that she was in control. There was just the right amount of mischief and ambivalence in her voice when she replied, "Maybe. . ."

All Eileen could do was shake her head sadly at her daughter's back, stubbing out her cigarette as Marie left the diner.

The scene shifted, and Robin was walking by the railing of the dam. Watching the water fall, it began to roar louder and louder. Suddenly, as though she were being pursued, she started to run through the woods. She ran into that stupid cop, back at the motel. Robin, panting and out of breath, sounded completely ridiculous as she tried to explain why she'd been running so fast. He calmed her down, and then went to his car and brought out a pair of hiking boots for her.

In response to her bewildered look as she held the boots in her hands, he explained, "In case you go hunting for any more crime scenes. . . Hope they fit."

Robin stared after him for quite a while as he was driving away.

The next part of the video was a replay of what I'd encountered in the Library—there was Dutton, with his Marquis de Sade book, and Marie in her spiked collar. Just hearing her yell "Sit!" at that poor dog was enough to make me jump again.

The last piece of video was of some brown-haired guy in a blue shirt running through the woods. He kept looking back over his shoulder, as if at a pursuer. There was an expression of fear on his face. I didn't recognize him at all, had never seen him in any of the prior scenes from the tape. As he ran, he seemed to get more and

more frightened, and slower and slower. Finally, he fell to the ground, clearly exhausted, and then I saw the figure of another man standing over him. While I watched, mute with horror, the figure took out the razor and then slit the throat of the man in the blue shirt. As the murderer stood up, I could tell it was Chuck. The dead man's head was between the bloody rocks. . . Then the screen went blank.

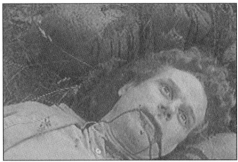

Chuck! So HE was the one committing the murders! But why? What possible reason did he have? Then I remembered Marie's expression when she handed him the straight razor, and understood at least a part of his reason. He was enslaved by her, in some way. I wasn't sure whether it was merely her sexual power that she held over him, or something more.

I was left to ponder that as I closed the GameBook. I had never been a religious person, but I got on my knees in the Chapel and prayed for help. I somehow doubted that my prayers could even get out of this evil house, but I felt better for doing it, anyway.

As I stood up, the clock chimed nine o'clock. Although the grandfather clock was at least several rooms away, it seemed to clang right in my very cranium.

CHAPTER FOUR

Nine O'Clock

The GameBook beeped, as always. I still had work to do.

Put an olive in a stein, mix it up, and get the equivalent of a fool's London subway. I knew that the London subway was a tube. A fool might be a boob. Did this mean I was looking for a boob tube? A television?

What did this have to do with an olive in a stein? Wait, mix it up. It was an anagram. *Another anagram. . . try "t" as the first letter.* An anagram of television.

I didn't need the rest of the clues at all: *Fool? Idiot? Moron? Boob!* and *London subway—the Tube?* and *Boob tube? A television?*

Just for form's sake, I checked the Map and noticed that the Attic on the "3rd floor.... and beyond" was hatched. So were the Kitchen on the first floor and three new rooms on the second floor—Mrtn. Burden, Jul. Heine, and Ham. Temple. But I was already headed back through the confessional door to Dutton's Room. I knew where the TV was.

When I touched the television, I was surprised to see a television in the GameBook. It was on the screen, and Robin's face was looking out of it at me. Or so I thought, as I anxiously pushed the play button.

It was less a television than a surveillance monitor. "Yes?" asked an off-screen female voice. It sounded strangely familiar to me, although I couldn't exactly place the voice.

"Samantha Ford?" asked Robin, in her 'professional' tone of voice.

"If you're selling anything, I'm not interested." So this was Samantha! I stared at her with a great deal of curiosity.

Samantha was a dark-haired, dark-eyed woman with a swift, if cynical, smile. Her voice had none of the small-town drawl that Eileen Wiley and the other Harley residents had. This was an educated, intelligent lady. And one who evidently didn't talk to strangers. "Please go away."

"No, I just want to talk to you." Robin was obviously standing at some kind of entrance to Samantha's home.

Why on earth did this woman have surveillance cameras outside her house, in a small, sleepy town like Harley-on-Hudson? Then I remembered that she, too, had survived some gruesome episode with the Stauf Mansion—". . . something's got her"— and I swallowed a lump in my throat.

Samantha was a skeptic. "About what?" she asked, impatiently.

"Eileen Wiley," Robin answered, simply.

This time, when the video screen went blank, I was frustrated and impatient, myself. I wanted to know more about this Samantha Ford. But that was for later, I guessed.

The GameBook was beeping. *A vital, instrumental part.* Were there any anagrams? I looked carefully, didn't see anything that stuck out.

A vital . . a living part? Perhaps I was a bit slow on the uptake. I shook my head, pressed the help key for another hint.

Are there any instruments in the house? Checking the Map, I saw that the Music Room was closed. Where else? That's when it dawned on me! The organ! That was a vital part!

A living part, an organ? I was off to the Chapel again, through Dutton's closet and that horrible, dripping corridor.

I touched the organ, and the keys played themselves with a jarring, ominous noise. It sounded as though someone had strangled a cat. I thought with a jolt that that was thoroughly possible, in this place.

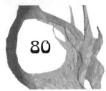

I opened the beeping GameBook to hear Stauf say, *"The number in New York is 22233642-736846873"* in a demented kind of chirping voice.

What was all this about? It was time for some help.

It's either a long telephone number or a code, or both.

Knowing how this place worked, it was more likely to be a code.

Telephones. Was it one of those codes based on the letters from the dial of a phone? If so, it promised to be tricky but not impossible.

Decoding the first number is academic. I tried it out, and sure enough, the first series of numbers spelled 'academic'.

Academics are said to live in one. The second series translated as 'penthouse'. Academic penthouse?

An ivory tower is a white castle. Ivory tower. White castle? Was this a literal castle—or more of a game? There was a chessboard in the Game Room. . .

But the Game Room, on the Map, was a solid blue. I had a hunch that more games might be found in the Attic, which was crosshatched on the Map. After all, the attic was where my family had packed away all our games, when we'd outgrown them as kids.

As I left Dutton's Room and headed across the corridor, I came upon a narrow door which led to another staircase, the one indicated on the Map. It would take me to the Attic. As I climbed the stairs, slowly and cautiously, bats swooped off of the ceiling and came too close to my head for comfort. The idea of being in the Attic here, at night, spooked me. I tried to remind myself that bats were actually harmless and interesting creatures—I remember we'd done a show on them once—but

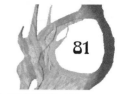

there were so many of them that I finally ran up the remaining stairs, unconvinced about the friendly nature of bats.

The Attic itself was fairly bare and not at all as ominous as I'd imagined. There was a lot of exposed wood, which was common in attics, of course, and the floors were hardwood. There were, however, some bloodspattered parts of the walls; I tried not to let them get to me.

I looked around. There was a tiny door, up some steps, at one end of the room. I didn't particularly want to investigate it. The Map identified the steps it as leading to The Room at the Top of the house.

To the left of this door, there was a toy train set on the floor. I went over to it and sure enough, it posed another puzzle. The little train had an engine, and was pulling compartment cars that were letters. The letters formed the name Faust. Well, that wasn't all that unusual, given the devilish goings-on in this house.

Manipulate the cars by switching between the top and the bottom track. Use the switcher.

The letters will spell out "STAUF". Faust and Stauf. Ugh, what an association. If my literary references were straight, though, it should be Stauf and Mephistopheles. More of a likely resemblance.

With some care, I finally got the train cars rearranged, using the little engine to push and pull them onto the side track, then back to the main

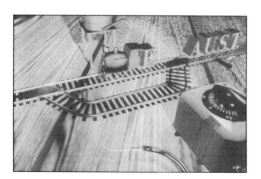

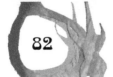

track. Eventually, the letters spelled Stauf. You'd think my ill-willed host would've been happy I spelled his name right. But he turned out to be more of a spoilsport.

As I stood up, I looked at the dress mannequin, fallen against the wall. As I went over to it to inspect it more closely, I noticed a chessboard with spilled pieces nearby. The only piece standing was a white castle. Or an ivory tower! I picked up the rook, and turned around abruptly. I wasn't alone in here!

There was a young woman in a black and white dress, crouched on the floor of the Attic. She had dark hair. Who was this? I went over to her, and she panted, "Please . . . Please don't hurt me. No, no more!"

I got down on my knees to help her. I reached out to touch her hair, in a comforting gesture. "I'm not goin' to hurt you," I said, trying to be reassuring. My hands only grabbed air. This was another ghost!

"Where's Eileen?" she asked me, panic in her dark eyes. This was Samantha! On the night. . . I couldn't go on. Something terrible had happened, that's all I knew.

I threw up my hands. How was I supposed to answer that one— "Eileen's a grown woman, who waits tables in the local diner?" Yeah, right. I had no idea what to say to this ghost of a scared Samantha Ford.

I answered truthfully, "I don't know."

Samantha went on as though I hadn't responded at all. "She ran away and left me . . . I couldn't move . . ." There was a wild look in her eyes.

" . . . something's got her," came into my mind again. Just at that moment, there was a scream from somewhere else in the house.

Samantha struggled to her feet. "That's her!" She ran off, saying sadly, "This is all my fault!"

And then the Attic was silent and still.

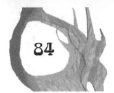

The beeping of the GameBook sounded harsh and somehow trivial in the silence that followed Eileen's scream. I opened it with a sigh, ready for the next clue.

Light piece from great orchestra. Light piece?

Or a piece that gives off light. In other words, this was another play on words.

The object needs to be illuminated in the last two words. The word is hidden in the words "great orchestra". I started to look. In a flash I saw it! The "t" at the end of "great" combined with the orch of orchestra spelled torch! That must be it! It's a torch!

There was an empty torch on the altar in the Chapel. I turned to leave the Attic, keeping a wary eye out for any more ghosts. Down the stairs, through the creaking wooden door and then I was back in Dutton's Room again. And soon I had returned to the Chapel.

As I touched the burned-out torch on the altar, it seemed to come to life for a moment in a small shower of red-orange sparks. There was the faint smell of gunpowder in the air, left behind when the sparks died out.

The GameBook showed a scene of Chuck pulling a corpse covered in a sheet out of the trunk of his car. He took it through the gates of the Stauf Mansion, and then across the field toward the house itself.

The macabre sight faded and I was left staring at the burned-out torch once more.

I answered the GameBook's beep and got the next clue. *Cheesy gadget that sounds larger.* It had to have something to do with cheese, I just felt that.

Um—something to cut the cheese? Asked my female ally. A knife?

If something's larger, it's bigger or greater. Sounds larger—sounds like greater? Grater? Was I looking for a cheese grater? *A cheese grater!* So that would be in the Kitchen, right? I consulted the Map. The Kitchen was next to the Dining Room, in the corner near the staircase where the grandfather clock stood.

Down the corridor I went, and I hurried down the stairs. As I entered the Kitchen, I wondered in a brief but desperate moment if this was really getting me closer to Robin. Were all my efforts really going to pay off, or would I be stuck in this rotting house forever, searching out objects and getting clues through a GameBook? I was beginning to feel like that Greek guy, the king who lived in hell and had to keep rolling a giant rock up a hill forever. Whenever he got the rock up to the top, it rolled down again and he had to start all over.

I was vaguely hungry, but that impulse faded as soon as I walked into the Kitchen. There was a smell, as of something rotting away. The whole room had an unsavory look to it, and I had the distinct sense that foul things had happened here, before. There was a butcher's block in the center of the room. It had a series of plates on it that looked too orderly in this random environment, where cleavers were stuck in cabinet doors and the old telephone hung, crooked, on the wall.

It must be a puzzle, I thought, and went over to it. Upon closer inspection, the plates were more like—I shuddered—eye balls. Naked and unstaring, but gelatinous-looking, all the same. They were arranged around a pentagram.

The object is to create five stacks of two plates on every point of the star pattern. A plate must jump two plates, stacked or not. Once moved, a plate cannot be moved again. This all seemed a bit confusing, but I thought I could master it if I tried.

A plate must jump two plates, stacked or not.

So perhaps I could jump a pile of two stacked plates as a move!

For my own convenience, I numbered the plates in my mind, starting with the plate at the top of the pentagram as #1. Various combinations sprung to mind; I tried a few of them out. Starting at different plates, jumping in different ways. Nothing seemed to work, though. I did find out that I could jump two plates, even if they were not next to each other. That was necessary to solve the puzzle.

Counting from #1, I found #8 and moved it over on top of #1. From there . . . well, I kept moving plates until I had two plates stacked on each of the points of the pentagram. Stauf was, as usual, a poor loser.

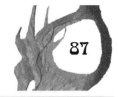

As I turned to my right, I saw the old wood-burning stove against a brick wall. There was a large kettle on it, and a bloodied cheese grater. As I lifted the grater, six severed fingers came out from underneath it, all moving in different directions like giant maggots. Horrified at the sight, I dropped the grater back onto the stove with a clang and backed away.

The GameBook beeped. I left the grotesque, dank little Kitchen before getting the next clue. *500 =100 = 0.* This was truly bizarre. What could it mean?

Try Roman numerals. Oh, great. Let's see—*D=500, and C=100.* But 0?

Wait, *D is C, Disc!* I had no idea what this was supposed to mean, but I knew that I needed to find a disc. There had been something in the Lab. . . Though I'd hardly considered it worth a glance, at the time.

The stairs were waiting. I went up them rapidly, and went down the musty corridor to Dutton's Room yet again. Through the Chapel, yes, and then into the Lab. On a small table next to the French door, I found what I'd seen out of the corner of my eye, earlier in the evening. It was a case for a CD-ROM game, called *The 7th Guest*. The name was familiar. I remembered Robin telling me about it, how it was based on the Stauf legend and all. Too bad I didn't have a computer around. Maybe, I thought, I could learn something by playing this game. After all, wasn't this whole experience nothing more than a game? A devious, twisted, and macabre game, but still nothing more than a game.

As I touched the case, it opened and I glimpsed the disc within.

The GameBook showed me a video of Samantha Ford at night, coming over in her wheelchair to see Robin at the motel. "I've come to tell you the truth," she said, "if you're ready for it." There was a certain grimness, a tension about her mouth.

Robin invited her in and the clip ended.

I opened the GameBook for the next clue. *Blend a TEAPOT SHOT and the pearlies won't rot.* I could see already that it was an anagram. Pearlies were teeth—it had to be toothpaste!

Teapot + shot is an anagram. No kidding.

Pearlies? Meaning teeth? I briefly allowed myself a really smug smile. For once, I was quicker on the uptake than my hinting friend. And I was on my way to the Bathroom, in search of the toothpaste.

When I touched the dab of toothpaste coming out of the tube, it suddenly turned into a writhing green insect. I cringed in repulsion and left the Bathroom. I was halfway down the hall when the next clue came through the beeping GameBook.

Slyness holding shipment in choppe? Lots of "S" words. And why was choppe spelled so strangely? It almost looked French. Or was it just a play on words? Well, now I didn't feel quite so smug about my rapid comprehension of these clues. I pressed the Help key, at a total loss. *Something else means sly . . . guile?* Guile?

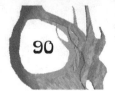
A holding shipment could be a "lot". Right. . . Hmm. Guile + lot. . . a guillotine!

To "choppe" someone? Well, a guillotine would choppe, all right! Inevitably, my mind went back to Eileen Wiley's missing hand.

Guile + lot + in = guillotine. With a shudder, I looked at the Map. Where might there be a guillotine? As I pondered the Map, it suddenly dawned on me how unlikely a household object a guillotine was! And yet, in the grips of this insane place, it seemed perfectly normal for me to be search for such an implement of execution! I shuddered again. Would I ever get out of this place? Would I be able to laugh at moments like this one, someday? It didn't seem all that likely.

Many of the second floor bedrooms were crosshatched; that is, I knew they still had secret puzzles for me to solve. I doubted that such a foul thing as a guillotine would be in a lady's room, although one couldn't really be altogether sure in this demented house!

I decided to head down the hall, to Hamilton Temple's Room and see what there was to see. The vague recollection that he had been a famous magician in his day, or something like that, came to me as I went down the hall. Robin's book had made some mention of it. Perhaps the guillotine I was looking for was less a tool of death than a kind of stage prop. I consoled myself with this idea, as I opened the door and stepped into Temple's Room.

It was a dark and Spartan room, though not overly creepy. There was the usual abandoned bedstead, only this one had the added feature of a dagger stuck in the headboard. Ghastly. There was a neglected painting, hanging crookedly . . . and to my immediate left, my flashlight illuminated a guillotine! To the left of the bed was a bookshelf. The bottom shelf contained a funny looking cube, and the cube was yet another puzzle!

As I looked at it more carefully, I could see that the cube was made up of dice, all stacked upon one another. There was a red arrow at the bottom left corner, and another arrow-thing at the top right corner.

You have to make a path from the starting die face to the ending one at the opposite side of the cube.

So, arrow to arrow. OK, that made sense.

The number of pips don't stand for numbers, they indicate direction.

The direction you choose defines the meaning of the die face from which you move.

As I understood it, then, I could pick any die, but once picked, that number would always cause the path to move in the direction I had used when I first picked it. I clicked on the first die face to the right of the starting point, one that showed the number four. From there, I moved to the right again, to the number one die. If I understood the puzzle correctly, every time the path hit a four from now on, it would move to the right, because I'd made the four go to the right, to the one. With that information, it wasn't long before I had traced a path from start to finish and Stauf was once again cursing me. What kind of a fool did he think he was dealing with, anyway?

Having solved the dice puzzle, I went immediately over to the guillotine and touched the blade. Of its own will, the blade raised up—I got my hand out of the way!—and slammed down into the cradle. Ghoulish. But not at all surprising. Perhaps I was getting used to things around here.

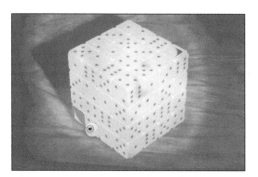

The GameBook was ready with another video sequence. I was ready to watch it, I thought. There was the gate to the Stauf Mansion closing, and a young Eileen Wiley came running toward it, trying to get out before the gate closed entirely. That's when it happened. The gate—I could hardly believe what I was seeing—seemed to come to life, and it closed on her hand. Not only did it close on her hand, it wouldn't let go! She started screaming, and blood streamed from her wrist.

Mercifully, the clip ended there. I didn't know how much more gory details about Eileen's hand I could take. I felt sick. And just moments before, I'd felt cocky and arrogant! I had almost forgotten the legacy of maiming and murder this house had created. And there's Samantha's story still to come, an inner voice spoke in my head, and that one promises to be even worse than Eileen's.

In a way, I was thankful for the GameBook and its scavenger hunt. At least finding all of those objects in the house gave me something to occupy my mind.

The book beeped. *Poor drainage could still produce a flower.* A flower, huh?

Drainage could make a flower if it's an anagram. Drainage? Was I looking for a flower in those letters?

Try starting with the letter "G," Gardenia??? Drainage is Gardenia! Although I was no gardener, I knew just where to find one.

I'd passed that painting at the top of the stairs so many times that I could probably sketch it out from memory. It had white flowers on it—I

Gamer's Note:

The door on the right in Temple's Room is a random door that leads to different locations within the house. The middle door leads to the Laboratory. Obviously, the left door leads back to the hallway.

was sure that one of them was a gardenia! I spun around to leave Temple's Room, and was truly shocked at what I saw.

There were three doors facing me. Where did they all lead? I hadn't seen three corresponding doors in the hallway. Which one led me back the way I'd come? I took the door to the left, and it took me back to the hallway. I wasn't sure where the other two would led, but I was glad I had guessed correctly.

I walked on up the corridor and stood in front of the painting at the top of the stairs. Well, it looked like a gardenia to me, that big white flower on the bottom of the bowl. I touched it, but nothing

happened. As I walked away from the painting, a terrible odor wafted from somewhere. It nearly made me gag, it was so noxious.

"Man, it stinks in here," I muttered.

From out of nowhere, a voice answered quietly, "Like that dead raccoon your father found in the basement . . ."

That's exactly how it smelled! How did he know about that? It was Stauf, wasn't it? For the first time since I'd entered this house, I was scared all the way down to my socks. Was I to be the next victim? How did he know things about me that nobody—nobody living—could know?

"Say what?" I asked aloud, aiming for a bold-sounding tone of voice. I pulled the GameBook out of my pocket. "You trying to tell me something?"

The GameBook wouldn't flip on. Nor was there any response to my question. With a sigh, I closed it. Wouldn't you know, the dumb thing beeped at me at that exact moment. "Why wouldn't you play when I needed you?" I asked impatiently.

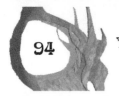

Then I concentrated on the clue at hand. *Sounds like it got higher from wine.* Sounds like. I knew enough by now to recognize a homophone clue.

What wine? Chablis, Fume, Rose, Burgundy? What did I know?

If you get higher, you rise. The other clue said "got higher"—past tense. Rose. Wine. Rose.

If you rise, you can say you rose! So I was looking for a rose. A rose?

It had to be in one of the rooms that had belonged to the women guests in the house. My destination, then, was probably Martine Burden's Room, which was the first door to the left, down the hallway from the painting. And that's where I went!

The first thing I saw in her room was a small round end table, with a curious-looking pyramid on it. Another puzzle, I wondered? It was a puzzle with letters. . .

You must reveal two fifteen letter words. Two of them, hmm? It sounded tricky.

Once a letter has been chosen, you may not pass through that letter's space again. Fair enough.

The outer corridor remains open. That seemed like a rule that might make it a bit easier, over all.

But now I needed to figure it all out. As I pressed on letters, they disappeared to form a word, at the base of the pyramid. I noticed that the whole process was like a labyrinth. As I chose a letter, often it would seem to "close off" the path. By using the outside part, I connected letters that seemed disconnected to one another.

Through a lot of trial and error, I determined to start on the letter "U," in the far right corner. The "N" next to it seemed like a pretty safe bet. Within a few moves, I could see what this word spelled—unintentionally. It was up to me to complete the puzzle, though, as best I could.

Once I'd managed to spell out "unintentionally," the game changed and a whole new set of letters appeared.

There was a "G," an "H," and a "T" in it. These had to be together. I searched the letters, trying to unscramble them. The word "straight" jumped out at me, and although I couldn't imagine what the next part of the word was, I went ahead and finished the word straight. That's when the rest became clear to me. I chuckled. A commentary on Martine Burden's character, perhaps?

I looked around the room. There was a bloody sheet on the bed. Wasn't this the one Chuck had brought to the house, wrapped around some stiff? It really wasn't something I wanted to think about right now. I had to find that rose.

There was a gripping painting on the wall, in grey tones, of what appeared to be the kidnapping of a young woman by some demon. I didn't like this at all. It reminded me somehow of Robin.

As I turned around from the painting, my flashlight shone on an old, moldy vanity. I continued around from there to another painting, this one more pleasant, though, of a nude woman. . . but wait! What was that flash of red? I looked back near the vanity, and there was a single rose in a vase right next to it.

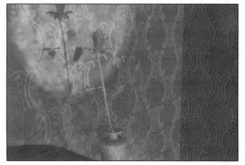

When I touched it, a petal fell off. I heard a feminine footstep behind me. "Robin?" I called out. I spun around to look, and there was a beautiful woman standing there. She had long hair, round shoulders and was wearing some kind of fancy velvet evening gown. Her earrings practically reached the base of her soft neck. The scent of roses filled the air around her.

She wasn't Robin, but somehow, as I looked into her eyes, I forgot all about Robin for a moment. "Wow!" I said, appreciatively.

The woman smiled at me coquettishly. "Oh, you like it?"

Were we talking about the dress? Or something else? I really wasn't sure. "Uh. . . yeah!" I stuttered.

"I hoped you would," she purred at me in her soft, seductive voice. Her perfume was overwhelming, so feminine and so vibrant, like a spring afternoon in the country. "I wore it just for you."

I didn't know what to say. "Well . . . thanks," I managed.

"So . . . do you think you have a role for me in your new play?" she asked, smoothing her hair back from her forehead in a fluid, almost feline gesture. A many-layered diamond bracelet flashed at her narrow wrist. I was mesmerized. But who did she think I was? And what was this about a play? "Do you think I'm right for the part?"

I threw my hands up. Was I dealing with an insane person? Of course I was. I began to consider. Who was this? She didn't live here,

did she? My brain felt foggy, slow-moving, all wound up in the mists of her perfume, which was changing even as she spoke. Now her scent was more like that of a waterfall in a deep forest. "Well, geez, you know, I. . . I don't know," I said, with an attempt at laughter.

"I'd be very grateful." Her voice was almost a whisper. I had to lean down to hear it. She put her gloved hand around my neck and pressed her head to my chest. Her perfume had changed again, the scent now cloying and intimate, winding its way around my olfactory more like a perspiring woman than a scent from a bottle. It was enough to drive a man crazy.

"Very grateful," she said, as she pressed her lips to mine. At that exact moment, her perfume changed again—and it was hideous, like something rotten, like putrifying wood, moldy fruit, something that had died a long time ago in our basement. The smell of death! It was all over her, and me, and I pulled away from that awful kiss with a start.

I realized that she must be one of the ghosts—perhaps even Martine Burden herself! God, how had I been so stupid? She had lured me. . . I wanted to get the lingering taste of death out of my mouth. I pushed her away from me, sputtering and gasping for breath.

"What's the matter?" she asked in a miffed voice. "You don't like me? You don't want me in your play?"

I didn't want to get any closer to her than I had to. The smell of her was choking me. But I certainly didn't want to go around pissing off any ghosts, either.

"Listen, it's not that I don't want you . . . in my play," I added hastily.

"I know I'm right for the part. . ." Her chest was heaving. She looked right through me with those big dark eyes. "I can give you more. . ."

"No. No, please. Could you just tell me where Robin is?" I asked, hoping to distract her attention. After all, if she lived here—she might even know.

Her miffed tone turned petulant. Like a child who can't have her way. "Who's Robin? What do you want with her? What's wrong with me?"

I started to say there was nothing wrong with her—but there was. Her skin had turned deathly white, and she was starting to fade away. . . turning into a black and white image like an old movie.

"Please, take me out of here," she pleaded. "Please, take me with you before—" She was fading fast, her voice cracking, burning away like old celluloid, but she was still pleading with me, "—before it's too late."

And that said, she faded into thin air. The malodorous scent faded with her, and only the faintest whiff of rose lingered in the room.

Conveniently enough, the GameBook checked in just then. Saved by the beep.

What kind of jewelry is angrier? I thought with a smirk that I'd never really known jewelry with an attitude. There must be an anagram in there, somewhere, though.

Angrier is the jewelry. It's an anagram. So angrier was the anagram, wasn't it?

Not pearls, but an earring. Of course. An earring!

Rummaging around Martine Burden's Room didn't turn up any earrings. It had to be in Julia Heine's Room, then. Well, I was just as

glad to get out of this god-forsaken room and head down the hall. I hoped Julia Heine wasn't going to show up, though.

Julia's Room was at the end of the hall to the left, next to the Game Room and opposite Hamilton Temple's Room. I made a beeline for a jewelry box I found in the corner, to the right of the bed frame. I opened the case, and there was another puzzle. This one was contained in the huge pendant I found there.

There were a number of multicolored hexagons, six of them to be exact, clustered around the central point. Each of the colored parts was some kind of inlaid stone. Very fancy.

Each gem must be adjacent to a gem of a matching color. So I had to turn them, or something, in order to make that happen.

You can rotate a cluster of gems, or swap positions with another cluster.

Again, I found that a numbering system came in quite handy. I called the top one #1, and went around clockwise. For starters, I just played around, trying different combinations. I discovered that when I touched one cluster, and then another, the two would change places. If I just touched the same cluster twice in a row, it would turn once, clockwise.

Myt first move was to exchange the positions of clusters #3 and #4, and then clusters #3 and #6. I swapped one more pair, then rotated a few times, and I had everything matched up. Oh, I had a few false starts,

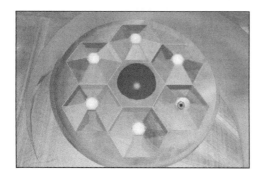 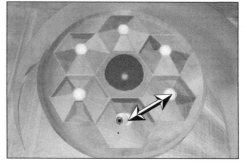

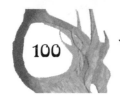

and my head hurt after I'd figured it out, but I experienced a sense of deep satisfaction when I heard Stauf's usual complaint.

That task done, I searched through the rest of the jewelry case, but couldn't find any earrings. Where could it be? My eyes lighted on the vanity, and that's where I found it, a little gold and black bauble with an enameled moon and stars.

As I reached out a hand to touch it, I heard Stauf say gleefully, "Now if we only had a matching ear!" A ghastly human ear appeared, bleeding from where it had been wrenched off of someone. The lobe was ripped clean through, as though the earring, too, had been wrenched from it.

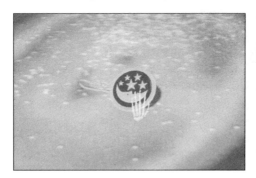

Amid Stauf's laughter at the gory sight, I felt a rage overtake me. I promised myself that I would get to the bottom of this, Robin or no Robin, and make this fiend pay for all he and his horrific mansion had done to innocent people.

Filled with that cold, calculating rage, I backed away from the vanity and answered the beep of the GameBook.

You might hear a well-mannered Cockney with a 60's hairstyle. I was completely in the dark. Well, in terms of this game, too.

Well-mannered is to behave. Behave? I was missing something. What did a Cockney have to do with this. Wait a minute. You might hear . . . did that mean another homophone?

The sound in Cockney makes a difference. Try it. At the urging of my unseen female ally, I did say it out loud. Behave sounded like behoive.

Hold it. Beehive! A 60's hairstyle! *Behave in Cockney sounds like beehive.* A beehive? Where was I likely to find one of those, here? Somehow, a beehive seemed like a stranger thing to locate in this house than a guillotine!

As I looked at the Map, I noticed that the Room at the Top, the one behind that mysterious little door in the Attic, was open for me to solve a puzzle. I had been in practically every other room in the house by now, and I certainly hadn't seen a beehive in any of them.

I hurried to the Attic, and made my way to the rickety stairs there, leading up to the little door to the Room at the Top. There was a stair missing, and the other ones didn't seem all too stable. I stepped really carefully, and went into the Room at the Top.

It certainly wasn't much like a room at all; more like the blasted out shell of what had once been an enclosure—some kind of garret. The windows were gone; in fact, most of the structure that would have held the windows in place was gone. The ceiling, likewise, was pretty much nonexistent except for a few beams. It was a real relief to be in the open air, anyway.

I looked around, taking in the bits of junk and broken toys that were scattered on the floor. I spotted the beehive in the corner.

The bees flew off of it as I came nearer, and left behind three drops of what appeared to be honey. There were also three drops of a red substance—was it blood?

    With shaking fingers, I opened the GameBook for some help. Try to end with more honey in the comb than blood.

    Globules divide in two when moved to an adjacent cell. But jumping the maximum of two cells moves the globule.

    Honey absorbs adjacent cells filled with blood and vice versa.

    This was the toughest puzzle Stauf had thrown at me yet, and for once, my ally in the GameBook was of little help. Damn Stauf, anyway. He was always one step ahead of me! But I persisted and eventually got the better of him. And oh, did that rankle. . . Too bad, Stauf. I'm going to beat you at every game you play.

    Well, that was finally finished. I sighed deeply, realizing for the first time how much defeating that puzzle had taken out of me.

    The GameBook came back up, and I knew it had a long, long video sequence to show me. I sat down on the floor of the Room at the Top, huddled against the wall, and got ready to fill in some of the blanks.

    Samantha was sitting in her wheelchair, typing furiously at a keyboard. The monitor in front of her—there were three of them in all—

had a view of the second floor of the Stauf Mansion! How was that possible? Samantha was able to track the inside of the house. . . it hit me like a ton of bricks. No wonder the voice of my invisible helper was so elusively familiar! It was Samantha. I didn't understand how or why this was possible, but it was the only explanation that fit.

She was one smart woman, and gutsy too. She was trying to help me. . . and Robin. Was she the one who'd sent me the GameBook? Had she somehow managed to create a video hookup to the Stauf Mansion? She must have. This was the first good magic I'd seen since I'd come to this town. The relief rushed over me.

There was a knock at the door, and I saw again the scene between Robin, outside, through the TV monitor, and Samantha. Finally, Robin came in, and, as usual, put her cards right on the table.

"I want to know what really happened the night you and Eileen Wiley went to the Stauf Mansion."

At the name of Eileen Wiley and the mention of the mansion, Samantha's face was frozen in some kind of reaction—I couldn't tell if it was fear or something else. She was inscrutable, though her eyes were like little dark stones, flashing out at Robin when the light hit them just right. She held, stubbornly it looked like to me, to the story that a dog had been responsible for Eileen's severed hand.

There was a pointed silence. Robin's tenacity seemed really pushy, to the point of obnoxious, to me. Samantha didn't seem to care for it much, either. She looked like someone trying to keep the lid on a lot of seething indignation, for the sake of politeness. But she was boiling underneath, even I could see that. When Robin asked what she was hiding, Samantha finally snapped.

"Who do you think you are, anyway? Coming here from some moronic TV show, speaking of the truth. You don't care about the truth. You care about ratings." Ouch. This lady fought fair, but she really knew where to hit.

As if perfectly aware of the accuracy of her jab, she continued softly, "Now ain't that the truth!"

To give her credit, Robin was pretty tough, too. I was actually enjoying watching these two strong women size each other up. They reminded me of martial artists, meeting for the first time, relentlessly polite but circling warily, each looking for the weak spot in the other. It wasn't often that Robin got as good as she gave. But Robin's style was subtle. She avoided the whole insult and tried to divert the other woman's attention by commenting on the monitors.

So much for subtlety. At that point, Samantha pretty much threw her out of the place. They were two highly focused women, each intent on getting what they wanted from the other. Robin wanted to hear the truth, and it didn't look as though she was going to leave until she heard it. And Samantha had clearly had enough of being badgered in her own home. She wanted Robin out of there, and now.

When Samantha wouldn't budge on the subject of Eileen and her hand, Robin tried another unsuccessful tactic. "What about you?" she persisted. Her voice was gentle, cajoling. "You haven't walked since that night."

I could tell from Samantha's shocked expression that she'd really had enough of Robin. She was all worked up, and practically shouted at

Robin to leave. She sat in the wheelchair, majestic in her anger, and held her ground.

Robin made as if to leave, but she couldn't resist turning around and getting one last word in. "It's been twenty years, Samantha. It's time you told the truth." Her face was severe. She turned back to the door and went out.

After Robin had left, the strength and resolve in this stone-faced woman seemed to crumble, as if she had finally succumbed to an inner pain greater than she could bear. She seemed to sink into her chair and become much smaller and more fragile than she'd appeared a moment before. Samantha leaned a weary head on her hand, and the scene faded to black.

Next thing I knew, I was watching myself in the Attic, meeting the traumatized ghost of a young Samantha.

This was all becoming like a bad dream from which I couldn't seem to wake up. There was Chuck, carrying that bloody-sheeted body into the Stauf Mansion. His lack of concern whether anyone saw him carrying a corpse in broad daylight was frightening. Where was that Chief of Police, anyway? Probably trying to get into Robin's pants, I thought scornfully.

I figured I'd seen all I needed to, but there was a part of the video I hadn't yet seen—Chuck set the body down on the threshold of the front door, knocked on the door, and then put the body inside. The door shut itself behind him. I thought I was going to throw up. He sacrificed a body to that house! Yet I'd seen no corpses in the house—ghosts, to be sure, and the bloody sheet on Martine's bed. I found myself incapable of speculating on the fate of that corpse.

The video rolled on, relentlessly. The next set of images showed Samantha rolling up to Robin's motel room and, a determined look on her face, saying she was ready to tell the truth at last. This was clearly not easy for her. I doubted whether she'd ever told the real story to anyone. She was risking a lot to come here and trust Robin.

Robin let her in immediately, and sat on the bed, opposite Samantha. If she was thinking this was going to be the investigative coup of a lifetime, it didn't show on her face. She exhibited a great deal of kindness and concern for Samantha. Funny how high-caliber women seem to treat each other better when the day is done, and they're not on their professional pedestals anymore. Or maybe Robin was just the cat who ate the canary and could afford to be gracious. She was, after all, going to get what she'd wanted all along.

Samantha was quiet, and serious. I wondered if she'd have the courage to speak. I found myself wishing her well. She was a brave lady.

The words fell out of her, deliberate and emotionally strained. "Everything that's happened since, every breath I take, is influenced by that night."

Robin, true to reporter form, stopped to record the whole thing. That girl didn't miss a beat!

The story Samantha wove, of the two young teenagers breaking into the house, in pursuit of a couple of teenaged boys, seemed innocent enough. Samantha portrayed herself as the wilder of the two girls, the one who'd talked Eileen into going along with the idea of breaking into the "haunted house."

"She did everything I did and. . . oh, God." Her voice trembled. "What happened to her. . . it was my fault."

Robin's solicitude was almost tangible. "Do you want to stop?" she asked, gently. Did she really care about Samantha, or was this just the right thing she thought she ought to say? I couldn't be sure.

The next words out of Samantha's mouth struck me as so bizarre I thought I must have heard them wrong. "We. . . we were raped."

By the house. Did I really hear that? Yes. I'm sure I did.

"Think what you want. . ." Samantha went on, a fierce light in her eyes, now, mingled with her tears. "But I'll tell you . . . that house is not what it appears to be. . . it's a living thing! It's a house or it's Henry Stauf or some ungodly creature. . ."

As she continued her story, of being held by invisible hands, and raped by an unseen creature, I really felt that the nightmare was unravelling all around me. I wanted out. I wanted out of this game. . . out of this house. As insane as it sounded, there was no doubt in my mind that her account was the truth. I was entirely aware that this house was a living, breathing entity. How else to explain all of the weird occurences here?

"I started screaming and Eileen got scared and ran." Tears were streaming down her face, by this point.

I saw Eileen again at the Stauf gate, screaming in agony as her hand was cut off by an unseen force.

There was no doubt about it. This was the most vile, gruesome story I'd ever heard, or even imagined. This, then, was the truth of what had happened in that mansion all those years ago. I felt an incredible sadness for Samantha and Eileen. Samantha's gut-wrenching honesty and her determination to tell her story through her tears and twenty years' worth of pain moved me beyond words. I didn't realize I was crying until I tasted salt in my mouth. But the macabre punchline was still to come.

"When it was finished with us, it simply let us go. . ." Samantha's eyes were swimming in tears. She pressed her hand over her mouth, as if to keep the pain from pouring out of her like a river breaking through a dam. Completely unselfconscious, she was crying even as she continued, "I got Eileen to Doctor Thornton . . . But the worst was yet to come. . ."

What could possibly be worse? I asked myself.

"Whatever it was—that thing—I. . ." the tears rolled down her face without her noticing, "I became pregnant. . . We both did."

"Oh my god . . ." Robin's horror was visible. Written all over her face. So was her pity.

Samantha had had an abortion. Eileen had been too scared to do so. The result of her back-alley abortion was that she was left in a wheelchair, with irreparable nerve damage as the result of an infection. My chest tightened at her pain, and my heart seemed to shrivel up inside it. It was unspeakable, what this poor woman had been through. And yet she was so beautiful, and so strong, and so capable.

At Robin's empathy about the horror she'd experienced, Samantha sat up straighter in her chair, and the woman who'd been practically sobbing a moment ago was gone.

"Eileen lives the real horror." Her voice was tense, her eyes were fierce. "She gave birth to Marie!"

More shocks. I wondered if there were any to follow—I wasn't sure I could stand many more.

"I'd rather spend my life in a wheelchair than have a child like that. . ."

Her description of Marie's inner evil was no surprise to me. But Samantha's claim that Marie was behind the murders. . . Well, I had suspected it, since I'd seen her slip the straight razor into Chuck's pocket, and yet I hadn't known it. Hadn't wanted to know, I guess.

Marie was the daughter of—a house? Evil incarnate? Henry Stauf? All of the above?

Samantha echoed my thoughts perfectly. "It's crazy. . . a house! Pure insanity. . . but it's the truth." Her voice took on a hard edge. "Just ask Eileen."

With that, she wheeled her chair around and left Robin's room.

After a brief pause, I saw myself again in the Stauf Mansion, talking to that voice that wasn't there. I heard a woman's giggle, and then I walked into Martine's Burden, looking for Robin. The scene with the attractive ghost of Martine played again. I shook my head at the memory. I must have been out of my mind, kissing a ghost.

Robin was back in the diner, having spoken with Samantha. Eileen didn't want to accept Robin's version of the story. Sassy as always, Eileen tried to bluff her way through the truth, though I distinctly saw tears in her eyes at at least one point.

"These two girls got pregnant," Robin was saying, "One of them had an abortion which left her

paralyzed. The other one had a daughter named Marie. . ."

Later on, regaining her composure, Marie's mother laughed scornfully. "That's just what it is. A story. How could anybody believe such a thing?"

But she was dealing with a professional, one who knew how to cut to the quick in order to get to the roots of a story.

"Is there any truth in what she says?" Robin asked, looking straight into Eileen's eyes.

There was a long pause. The muscles around Eileen's mouth were engaged in some kind of struggle. Her mouth worked for a moment, pulling this way, pulling that way, before she finally mastered herself and said "No."

It was obvious to both of them, and to me, that Eileen was lying.

"What is it about this house, Eileen? What's it really all about?" Robin's tone was pleasant enough, but there was an undercurrent of urgency in it, too.

Eileen Wiley smirked. "Why don't you just go there yourself?"

At Robin's lack of response, she taunted softly, "You're afraid, aren't you?"

Was she? Speechless for once in her life, Robin got off the stool and strode out of the diner. Eileen watched her go.

A young woman sitting in the booth directly opposite the diner counter whipped her head around. It was Marie. She glowered at her mother and her look said, "Don't you dare, or I'll chop you down like

any other weed in my way." Eileen was a proud woman, but her expression at that moment was a frozen mask of mingled fear and resignation, that of a deer caught in the headlights.

Gamer's Note:

Some people may wonder how Samantha has managed to monitor the interior of Stauf's mansion, and why. The answer is that Samantha is a computer whiz who has tapped into Stauf's own surveillance system. Basically, she's hacked Stauf, and is dedicated to bringing an end to his evil.

CHAPTER FIVE

Ten O'Clock

When the video was over, my legs were stiff from sitting on the cold floor of the Room at the Top. I closed the GameBook and stood up, thinking. The chiming of the grandfather clock roused me from my reflections about Marie, Samantha, Eileen, and Robin. It was ten o'clock. I had learned a lot in the last hour, but I still wasn't any closer to finding Robin.

Then the GameBook beeped, and I was off on another wild scavenger chase.

Instrument is sharp, but is missing its head. Was there an anagram?

Missing its head . . . missing the first letter? When I heard Samantha's voice, I was filled with gratitude and sadness, all at once. Too bad I couldn't let her know how much I appreciated her help.

The instrument is not missing the first letter. Just what kind of an instrument was I looking for, anyway? A knife? A musical one?

Take the "S" out of sharp!

Oh . . . I finally got it. I was looking for a harp!

I looked at the Map. A harp would probably be in the Music Room, I reasoned. I sighed. I had a few flights of stairs to go down to get there. When I opened the door to leave the Room at the Top, a huge bat flew right at my face. It was unnerving. I would sure be glad when this was all over.

The Music Room was a dilapidated sight. The once ornate carpet was damp and rotting in places, and the panels of the walls were molded and mottled. There was a piano in the center of the room, its keys broken and missing, and a harp in the corner. Things were strewn around on the floor; sheet music, a bust of someone I thought was Beethoven, a tumbled chair, a discarded violin on the floor. It was a mess.

On the the fireplace mantel, there was a small game, between the candlestick and the clock. It seemed to be a small grouping of furniture, with a piano in the middle. The red arrow on the right side was curious.

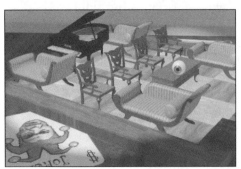

Upon consulting the GameBook, I learned that the point of the game was to move the pieces around until you can move the piano off the board. Was this for real? That sounded impossible!

Even Samantha seemed to understand my reservations. *This one's difficult.*

I can't tell you how long I spent trying to figure this puzzle out. Eventually, I'm not even sure how, I did solve it. I managed to get the piano off the board by moving all the chairs and couches out of the way. It was not easy, and I enjoyed Stauf's usual conciliation speech all the more because of it.

As I turned around in the Music Room to go to the harp, there was an empty space in the center of the room where the grand piano had been!

Shaking my head at this peculiar result of the furniture game, I went over to the harp and touched a string. It played itself for a moment, a haunting chord. I stepped back, and the GameBook beeped again.

A defective truck with a crane makes for a ball-busting ballet. Baffled, I went to the help key.

Truck and crane . . . came Samantha's soothing voice. An anagram.
Start with letter "N"! OK, but what did this have to do with a ballet?
Aren't, er, balls called nuts? I could hear her blush to say it!
So maybe the first word in the real word was nuts.
If you bust something, it cracks! Oh, of course! Now I saw it! A nutcracker!

Hadn't I seen one of those, somewhere? In a place that I went through a lot. . . of course. The hallway! I'd seen it on the floor, in the

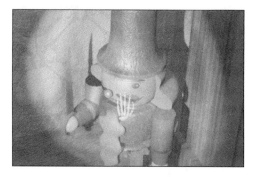

corner down at the far right end of the hall, beyond the lion sculpture. It was near the Game Room door.

Sure enough, the little wooden figure, brightly painted in reds and blues, was there just as I had remembered. When I touched the nutcracker, its jaw opened and closed, and its little sword arm went up and down with a squeak, as if it were animated from within. Spooky. But normal for this house of horrors.

When the nutcracker stopped its motion, the GameBook popped up with another piece of video. It looked to be a scene between Marie and Chuck. I could hardly wait to watch this one. I pushed the play button.

There was Marie in a motel room, one that looked a bit like Robin's. Chuck came in, all happy-go-lucky. It made me sick. How could a murderer be so jolly? Even if he was doing Marie. Especially if he was doing Marie!

All excited, like a puppy, he said, "Hey, Sweet Marie!"

She pulled out a knife and grinned an inhuman grin, at once menacing and mischievous. "It's that time again."

Chuck looked appalled. OK, so maybe he did have a conscience after all. "So soon? But Marie, I— " Or maybe he was lazy.

"Shut up!" she interrupted him. "Just take this knife and get that TV producer."

The video was over. I realized I was staring at the toy nutcracker's little sword. There was a new chill running through my veins.

The GameBook was ready with another clue.

Look at key missing first misprinted label. Huh? That one wasn't even English.

But Samantha was there to untangle it for me. This is two clues!

Look at "key" missing first . . . letter? *Key without "K" was ey.* What was that supposed to mean?

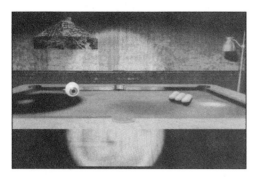

Misprinted label . . . a mixed up word? So label was an anagram, huh? I looked, but couldn't really find a word in it. I kept seeing ball, but there was an extra "E". . . wait a minute!

"Ey" plus "eball" equals eyeball. So it does.

An eyeball. Hadn't there been a little ball on the pool table? I went into the Game Room, curiously, and looked on the pool table. There was a miniature cue ball, painted like an eye. I gave it a spin and was pretty revolted by the sight of its back—it was like an eyeball cut out of the head, complete with the nerve canals and blood around them! How appropriate. . .

I drew back from the pool table, and the GameBook beeped at me. *Disabled cutting edge.*

Disabled . . . maybe the word itself? Was it another anagram? *Lose the prefix to disabled.* That would just leave abled. Abled unscrambled was blade! So the part about a cutting edge made sense.

I'd seen so many blades in this house I couldn't tell which one to go find. There was the cleaver, stuck into the wall in the foul-smelling Kitchen. I'd rather not go after that one, thank you very much. Then the nutcracker's little sword. Marie had knives, too, plenty of them. Not to mention her straight razor. . . was I losing my mind? Confusing video of the past with the events of the present? It was the effect of the house, I was sure. But no, I'd seen a straight razor, too, in the Bathroom. Then there was the dagger impaled in the headboard of a bed—had that been in Hamilton Temple's Room? It was too confusing. Which one of these would it be?

I would have to search every one of them, I thought grimly. I was in the Game Room. Hamilton Temple's Room was the closest to me. I'd start there.

As I looked closer at the dagger impaled in the bed, I noticed it had a curiously-shaped handle, for gripping. Some kind of a hunting knife. Well, we were all being hunted, all right. I touched it for a moment, and then knew I'd found the right item in this strange treasure hunt.

The GameBook came up, with another piece of video. Chuck was at the motel. He pulled the same exact knife from underneath his jacket— at least it looked identical. He walked into a room. Was it Robin's? Robin was lying in her bed; I could see her hair on the pillow. In a quiet but quick moment, he plunged the knife down toward the bed. My heart pounded in my chest. The video stopped there.

But Robin had called out to me after this had all happened. Hadn't she? Even now, I supposed, she was in that damp crypt-like place, with the water-creature trying to pull her in. If Chuck had killed her, how was this possible? My logic wasn't all that reassuring in this place.

What if Robin was already dead, and I was hearing her ghost? Or if the house had been trying to lure me into it. . . These were the imaginings of a paranoid. The house had plenty of local blood to drink, it didn't need to summon mine all the way from Connecticut. Besides, Samantha had sent me the GameBook, had shown me images of Robin calling out for me. Samantha wouldn't play me false. Would she?

But Chuck had lunged with the knife. He must have hit something— or someone—unless he was a total incompetent. Replaying his lunge in my mind, he didn't strike me as an incompetent.

What had really happened? I figured there was only one way to find out. And of course, the GameBook beeped, as if to answer me, "Yes. That's how!"

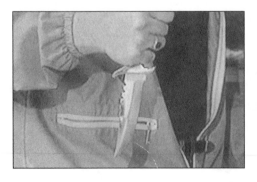 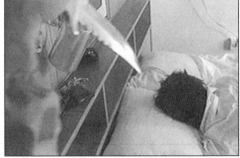

Unreasonable reason. This was obviously another word-game. I seemed to have lost my taste for games.

A reason . . . a motive? A motive? Well, OK, Samantha, if you say so. You haven't steered me wrong yet.

Unreasonable . . . what—nut . . . loco . . . crazy? A crazy motive. So far as I could tell, every motive around here was wacko.

A locomotive. Of course! The train! I took the left-most door out of Hamilton's Room, and raced up to the Attic once more. I touched the train, and for a few demented seconds it seemed that I was on the train track, and the train, its light on, was rushing right for me!

I shook my head. I'd been in this house way too long. I backed away from the toy train set, and opened the GameBook for the next clue.

Paper used in unusual theses. Unusual theses . . . mixed up theses? Was "theses" an anagram? *It's some kind of paper.* I was thoroughly confused.

Unless . . . *"theses" mixed up is "sheets"! But not sheets of paper in this case.* Could it be bed sheets?

I'd seen that bloody sheet in Martine Burden's Room. I had also seen a sheet of parchment paper in Martine's Room, but it wasn't paper, right? Checking the Map, I noticed that the room called the Doll Room was crosshatched. Now, when did that happen? I'd want to check that out later.

In Martine's Room, the note was on the window sill, but that wasn't what I was looking for. On the bed, I noticed again how the blood had seeped into the mattress. I was reminded of the video I'd just seen, of Chuck stabbing someone in the motel bed. I touched the sheet, as far away from the bloody patch as I could. Nothing happened. I touched every possible part of the sheet. Nothing happened.

Finally, I understood that I'd have to touch the bloody piece of the sheet. There was no other choice left to me. Hesitantly I brushed it with my fingers. Horror of horrors—it was warm and wet! How that could be,

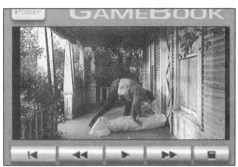

I had no idea. I didn't particularly want to know, either. Hastily, I brushed my bloody finger off on a clean piece of sheet.

I settled down to watch the next piece of video in the GameBook. It began with Chuck, stuffing that bloody corpse into the door of the house again. Or maybe it was a different corpse, because it was a different corpse, because Chuck was pulled into the house right behind it! That looked to me like the end of Chuck. Maybe he had been just a little too relutctant to follow dear Marie's last deadly command. . . .

When the video ended, I had the grisly feeling that more awful circumstances would unfold before this was all through. The house's rape of Eileen and Samantha was almost peanuts compared to Marie's actions. I had the sense that I only knew the half of it! There was so much evil in this house! Even now, I could feel it pulsing and breathing around me, watching me and waiting—for what?

The GameBook had been beeping for some time before I really noticed it.

Adroit holding a sharp instrument. I sighed. Another blade, no doubt. Which one was it, this time?

If you're adroit, you're handy, smart, clever . . . Where was this leading? I couldn't be sure.

There are a lot of sharp instruments lying about. You could say that one again, Samantha.

Clever holding "A"? Hmmm. Clever with the letter "A" equals Cleaver. So, this time it was the cleaver. This didn't mean that I was going to witness another ghastly murder, this time perpetrated by someone holding a cleaver, did it?

Back in the Kitchen, I grasped the handle of the cleaver imbedded in the door. All by itself, it pounded into the wall, wood chips flying from it.

When it stopped, I heard a louder rapping than the cleaver in the wood. I spun around, and there was a white-haired woman pounding a cleaver on the butcher's block. I couldn't exactly see what she was pounding. Wasn't sure it was a good idea for me to, either. By her dress and her pearls, I figured this must be Julia Heine. She was

really in the room, though, I'd be willing to swear it—she didn't shimmer like some of the other ghosts I'd seen in other places in the house.

The sight of a bemused-looking Chuck standing behind her was a real shock to my system. It looked as though he was equally shocked to be confronted with Julia.

"Hello, Chuck," she said ominously. Her singsong diction reminded me of Katherine Hepburn in *The Philadelphia Story*. But there was something dangerous in her voice. "Are you ready?" she continued.

Chuck was clueless. He obviously didn't know what was going on, or why he was there. He just looked stupid, which, I suspect, was a natural state for him.

Just then, another man entered the room, and I recognized him instantly from pictures in Robin's old files. It was Stauf, himself. For the first time, I got a look at the fiend behind all the misery and death. He was quite jolly, as if he was having the time of his life. Or death. Or whatever.

"Soup's on," Julia said, and Stauf echoed her.

Then, I swear, the pot of soup on the stove suddenly came to life and a grotesque skull shape emerged from it. And, believe it or not, it also said, "Soup's on."

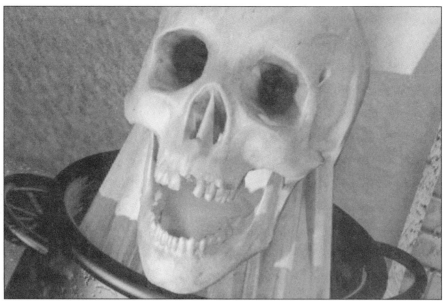

Poor Chuck. If he hadn't been such a fool, I would have felt sorry for him. He stood there shaking his head, as if this couldn't really be happening to him! How quickly the tables turn, eh Chuck?

Then Julia, Stauf, and the soup all started making Chuck jokes. It was macabre. Then Julia came toward Chuck, who started to back away. I had forgotten about the cleaver. She raised it high, Chuck screamed, Stauf looked excited, and it was the end of this strange moment or vision, or whatever it was. I know it was a pretty sick thought, but I found myself thinking I wouldn't want to have any soup for supper in this house. I hardly felt a lot of remorse for Chuck. Dupe or not, he had murdered several innocent people. In fact, for all I knew, he might have murdered Robin. That sobered me and my mood instantly changed.

The GameBook broke me from my moment of morbidity. With a sigh, I opened it and got the latest clues in this twisted, dirty little game.

A desserted Arthropod. The cake shaped like an insect! I'd seen it on the Dining Room table, and had been instantly disgusted by it.

I didn't even need the hints from Samantha, but I thought I'd check them out, anyway, just to be safe.

Desserted is misspelled. Or is it? I doubted it, as I figured we were talking about a cake.

An arthropod could be a crustacean. An arthropod abandoned by natural selection could be one that is extinct. No arguments with the science lesson, here.

Desserted could mean "made into a dessert." I knew it! That cake!

One extinct arthoropod is a trilobite. So that thing on the table wasn't an insect—it was a trilobite! An extinct creature, which was what I was afraid I was going to be before this was over.

I ran into the Dining Room and checked out the trilobite cake on the table. It was another game!

 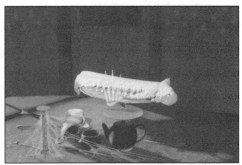

Get four of your bon bons in a row before Stauf does. So that's what those weird little lumps were! Bon bons. They didn't strike me as all that appetizing. God only knew where they'd been!

Drop a new bon bon onto a stack by selecting a vertical section of the trilobite. Hey . . . this was a lot like a game I'd played as a little kid!

The bon bons can be connected vertically, horizontally or diagonally. Watch out for those diagonal connections, Samantha warned, *they can be hard to see.*

I played for a while, until I got the hang of it. Setting up ways to get four in a row from more than one direction seemed to get Stauf's goat. It didn't take me all that long to beat him.

And then the GameBook came up with the long video. There was Marie, pacing restlessly around the motel room, again, and Chuck came in, just as I'd seen before.

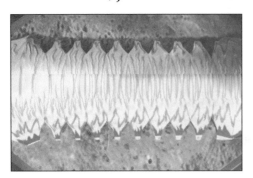 

When Marie told him to kill Robin, Chuck revolted. "Oh, no, Marie. I can't do that, not her."

They were both nervous. She was practically hysterical, as she screamed at him and threatened him with some dreadful consequence if he didn't do what she wanted him to.

"You know what'll happen to you if you don't!" she shrieked.

I really didn't know what that was supposed to mean, though having seen Julia Heine's treatment of him, I had a pretty good guess. I wonder if Chuck really knew what he was up against.

As she raved at him to kill Robin, he tried to reason with her.

"Marie, just listen to what you're saying."

"No," she practically screamed at him, "YOU listen! Do you really want to say no to Stauf?"

She had a point there. Chuck capitulated, however reluctant he may have been to kill Robin. He tried to feel Marie up, but she pushed him away, saying they could do that later. Finally, he left, and she was alone in the motel room.

She closed her eyes for a second, in relief. Almost lost your hold on him, there, eh, Marie? Or so it looked to me. Marie exhaled, a deep sigh.

And the scene changed. It was Chuck, once again stalking Robin in her motel room. I saw the scene with the knife again. He plunged it in and. . . Wait. That's not Robin. Is it? It's. . . it's Chief Jim. In her bed. Oh, my God.

I was completely awash in conflicting emotions. I was relieved it wasn't Robin—that was first and foremost. But there was only one possible explanation for this guy's presence in her bed. I felt sick to my stomach at that. Although it shouldn't have been a complete surprise, the way they'd been acting all along. Now I understood why she'd called out for me, I thought cynically. One knight in shining armor was dead. Call another.

Jim was dead! It was horrific. On the other hand, he wasn't going to be doing her any more.

And finally, I now understood why Chuck had fed the soup pot. He had not only resisted orders, but he had killed the wrong victim. So, Chuck. . . was toast. And he knew it.

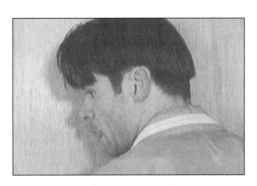

Well, as I watched, I saw Chuck listen at the bathroom door. Robin was in there! Taking a shower! Chuck set about removing the knife from the body, which he had a lot of difficulty doing. It was stuck. Despite everything I had seen up to now, the sight of Chuck yanking and tugging on that knife struck me as truly macabre. Giving up on the knife, Chuck grabbed all the Chief's stuff and wrapped it up with the body in the sheet. Did he think Robin wasn't going to notice that not only was Jim gone, but most of the bedding as well? Or did he care?

Of course, Chuck's fingerprints were all over the place, but I guess that doesn't matter, now.

Robin came out of the bathroom moments after Chuck had left with the body, wrapped in a towel. "Jim?" she called, a confused look on her face.

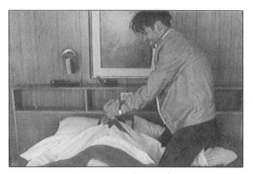

The scene shifted again. There was Chuck trudging up the hill toward the old house, a body carried with familiar ease over his shoulder. Practice makes perfect.

The look on Chuck's face as he neared the house was that of one worried murderer. Yes, I think Chuck wasn't sure what old man Stauf was going to do about this.

Well, I already knew, and the next scene repeated Chuck's last stand. It was a souper scene. Hmm. Maybe I'd spent too much time in that house. Anyway, after Julia and Stauf had carved up Chuck, the scene changed again, and this time it showed something I hadn't seen before. It was Robin. And she was at the Stauf Mansion.

Robin slowly got out of her car. She walked tentatively toward the huge gate and stared up at the sign that read "Stauf." With a determined look in her eye, she went inside the gate. I could tell she was scared. Robin was fighting her fears, and it showed.

In the last shot of Robin that I saw, she stood silhouetted against the Stauf Mansion. It didn't take a genius to guess that the next bit of video would have shown her entering the house and falling into its grim clutches.

CHAPTER SIX

The Eleventh Hour

The clock struck eleven o'clock, and I knew that this was truly the eleventh hour. I had a lot to do before midnight. I scarcely had time to consider all that I'd seen in the long video sequence. I really wanted to get out of here.

The friendly GameBook beeped. I flipped it open, ready for another clue.

663 264625 46 2 6455466. Another telephone dial coded message?

Is there an animal in a word here? Let's see. I thought I saw the word animal, itself, as the second one.

It's another number substitution cryptogram. It spelled out. . . "one animal in a million."

The animal is in the word "million." Huh?

Take away "mil" and it leaves "lion." Lion! The sculpture in the hallway, at the top of the stairs!

I stood over the lion, and almost hesitated to touch it. What fresh atrocities would be revealed to me?

I had a moment of vertigo, and few seconds of disorientation, then there was Robin, walking down the hallway with her back to me. As she turned around, there was Stauf's voice saying silkily, "You don't like cats, do you, Robin?"

"Who's there?" she asked, worried. It was the same trick he'd played on me, the bastard. Using my past to intimidate me, throw me off guard.

"You've been afraid of them ever since you were a little girl," he continued in a smarmy tone of voice, "ever since you and your sister drowned the kitten in the toilet."

"How did you know I—"

"Poor little kitten." The voice of mock regret.

"I didn't mean to drown it," protested Robin.

Stauf persisted softly, "Poor little dead kitty. Here, kitty, kitty."

Then there was a cougar, a live one, at the end of the hall. Robin froze in fear. It walked over to Robin slowly, stalking her, and then, as I cringed helplessly, it sprung at her as though she were a mouse. Its wild

snarling was enough to make me cover my eyes. Her hands were in front of her face, braced for the blow.

And the screen went dead.

Damn him! I thought bitterly. He'll use anything, anything. He's just toying with us. In this house, we really are just mice. And Stauf is the cat.

The GameBook was ready with the next clue.

Drink left at sea. I was too distressed by the sight of Robin having been attacked by that cougar. I couldn't seem to think straight.

A nautical term? I wasn't a boating man, myself, so I wasn't sure what it was.

Not starboard. Oh, port.

Left on a ship is port. Had I seen any port, anywhere?

It must be in someone's bedroom. Probably one of the masculine rooms. I'd been over Martine Burden's room pretty thoroughly, and Julia Heine's as well. I paused for a moment at the thought of that cleaver. Whew. There wasn't any port in Dutton's room, I was sure of that. Nor Temple's, for that matter.

I hadn't been over Knox' Room with a fine-toothed comb. That seemed like the logical place to look. There was a nautical skeleton on the mantel, tied to the wheel of a ship. I was definitely on the right track.

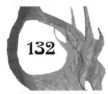

A wine glass stood on a table next to the bed. I went over and picked it up.

Edward Knox stood before me in the room. I assumed it was he, anyway; an older gentleman in a tuxedo. He was considering the glass in his hand. All in all, he acted startled to see me.

"Oh—sorry. . . didn't see you come in." At least his demeanor was fairly jovial. "Just sampling something from Stauf's cellar. Would you—?"

He interrupted himself, before I could react. "I guess not. After all, you don't have time for that, now do you?"

What was that supposed to mean?

"You're looking for her." He winked as if he were on my side. "I know—we all know that— but you see. . . someone's coming for YOU. You can't get out— have you tried the front door. . . It's quite impossible. . ."

He started squirming around, looking acutely uncomfortable. "And now—you'd better—hide!"

I barely had time to wonder what he meant by that as his head swelled up. No, I mean it really swelled up, to the point where it looked as though it were going to burst—and it did!! Just like that, it exploded, sending jagged bits of brain and eyeball and tongue flying about the room! Instinctively, I drew backward, ducking and covering, half expecting to be splattered in gore. And then he was gone, leaving me to stare at the half-filled glass of port again.

I shook myself to get my wits about me. I had long since ceased to feel much lasting concern over the cruel and horrifying antics of these talking halucinations, but they seemed quite real in the moment. After taking a few deep breaths and checking my clothing of any stray bits of shredded flesh and chunks of grey matter, I consulted the GameBook, which was beeping again. I had the feeling this ordeal was going to come to an end soon. I just hoped it didn't mean that I would come to an end, too.

Snake, baby, trap. Were there anagrams?

A type of snake? Was it a word play?

Something a baby uses? I was no expert on baby needs.

These words have something in common. Yeah, I thought savagely, they're all obscure and unconnected. But I kept my mouth shut. After all, Samantha was trying to help me!

They all can be combined with "rattle". Rattle? Was I looking for a rattle?

The Map said there was a Nursery in the house. But how did one get there? Or maybe the rattle was in the Doll Room. I hadn't really been in either of those two rooms yet.

At any rate, I set off down the long corridor, to the Doll Room. The hallway got really narrow. It was covered in some grimy goop that gave off a foul smell. I didn't want any of it on my clothes. Like so many other things in this dreaded house, the mold itself seemed to be alive and breathing.

The Doll Room was not as charming a place as its name might suggest. Sure, there were dolls in here, and other toys as well, but they were all worn out and dilapidated and kind of ominous-looking. I found an old-fashioned bureau, and saw a wooden puzzle on it. Obviously, I wasn't going to get anywhere in this room until I tackled this latest Stauf challenge.

There were chess bishops, two white and two black, standing on a network made out of tinker toys. What the?

"You can tinker with it all you want," chimed Stauf, "but you won't solve it!"

I didn't believe that for a moment. What did Samantha have to tell me? *Interchange the white bishops on one side with the black bishops on the other.*

You can move any piece in any order, but it must move along a straight line, and not land in line with a bishop of the opposite color.
I think I can do it in 18 moves.
I found the bishops would slide on the diagonal along the axes of the tinker toys. I had to start and restart a few times. Finally, I began with the white bishop in the back and moved it diagonally forward. Then I moved the front black bishop three spaces. And. . . well, ultimately I did solve this puzzle in 18 moves, just as the clue had indicated. Stauf, as usual, wasn't amused. By this time, neither was I.

Now, where was that rattle? I couldn't find it anywhere in the room, but I did discover some floor boards that felt loose to the left of the bureau. My flashlight picked up some kind of space between them, near the wall. As I went over to get a closer look at the spaces, there was a bit of light coming up through them. Upon even closer scrutiny, I realized that two of the floorboards were sealed together in a way that resembled a trap door! I slid them back, over to the right, and jumped down into a hidden room.

A quick look around was enough to tell me that I was in the Nursery! I had found it, quite by accident.

The Nursery was another cold, damp room. The walls were dripping with moisture, the wallpaper ruined. In many places the walls had been scribbled upon! There were childish sayings and sketches and all kinds of weird writings and scrawlings on them. I searched the room, overturning old musty toys, until I found the rattle.

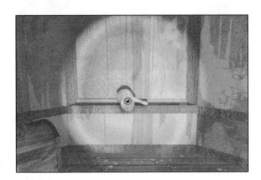 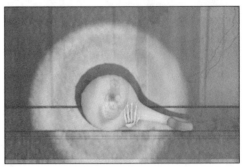

When I touched the rattle, it jumped off of the ledge by itself and shook. If this was any kid's rattle, I decided, it must have been Marie's. The thing was demented and shook itself.

Robin stood in front of me, in the Nursery. I couldn't talk to her, and I knew that I was again witnessing a scene that had already happened. Her face was bleeding from a long scratch, and her shirt was torn. She looked pretty forlorn as she wandered around the Nursery.

As she picked up a baby-doll and looked at its little face, it turned into something demonic—complete with long fangs—and cried out, "I want my mommy!"

Revolted, Robin dropped the nasty doll as though it were on fire.

"I want my mommy," came a mimicking voice from behind Robin. "And what do you want?" asked Henry Stauf, at his most urbane. "Not your mommy . . . I'd guess. . ."

"Who are you?" Robin looked more bewildered than scared. She really didn't know who he was. Then again, she hadn't seen what I had seen—had no real reason yet to fear this lunatic villain the way I did.

Stauf went on, unheeding, "Success. . . power. . . influence. . . money. . . fame. . . Some of us want even more than that. . ."

Although he reminded me of a snake, hynotizing its victim with its eyes, he was certainly on a roll with this sincerity number. "I thought that all I wanted was money, enough wealth for, oh, a lifetime or two. . ." He reached out and touched a strand of her hair, and Robin shrugged his hand off in annoyance. Stauf seemed not to notice.

"But that was only the beginning," he continued as he stooped to pick up the doll—Robin's eyes were fixed on it as he spoke. "And all that

IT wanted—all the house wanted in return, was merely to exist. But, of course, like so many things, to exist it needs to be fed—"

"What are you talking about?" Robin's face was a mixture of shock and confusion. And disgust. Aha. She'd pegged him for a looney.

His expression became harsh, his tone severe. "To live it must eat. That's not so much to ask, now is it?" His eyes were like daggers, piercing her. Her whole body tensed as he came near. I noticed that my own hands were shaking.

The terse intensity in his voice faded abruptly, and he was again the picture of urbanity. He searched her face. "And what is it that you want. . .? What can this house—my house—give you? Success . . . power . . . influence?"

"How can a house give anything to anyone?" She was openly derisive.

"Never doubt the power of this house," Stauf intoned like some kind of evil sorcerer, invoking the demon-deity he served. "You've seen its magic."

"You're saying I can have anything I want. . .?" She was trying to get this straight. I couldn't tell whether she thought he was just a nut, or someone making a legitimate offer.

"Name it," Stauf proclaimed in an off-hand, grandiose way. He turned away from Robin with a nonchalant smile. He thought he had her, I could tell. The bastard. Did he really think it was that easy?

I was waiting for Robin to tell him where he could stick his bizarre offer. But I didn't get the chance to see that. The video was over.

The GameBook beeped.

A letter from Greece is quite a number in Rome. This was some twisted play on words, I could tell that right off the bat.

The letter is not a missive. Not a written letter. Hmm. So we were talking about some kind of alphabetic letter?

The 24th letter of the Greek alphabet. It was all Greek to me. What were the later letters. . . pi, thi. . .I couldn't really remember.

In Rome it is eleven. Hey, wait a minute! The Roman numeral eleven looked like. . . It is XI. Now where have I seen that? Only on a clock, I mused.

Of course! On the face of the grandfather clock!

There was a door on one wall of the Nursery. I took it, and found to my surprise, that it led back to the Doll Room!

I ran out into the hallway and went down the stairs, found the clock, and touched the number XI on its face.

I was able, much later, to piece together some of the events that happened next, though I was only present for some of them. Samantha Ford was watching the entire scene between Robin and Stauf on one of her monitors. Stauf was pushing Robin for an answer to his diabolical offer.

Robin said haltingly, "I—"

Samantha became frantic. "No, don't say it!" she cried.

She typed frantically, her eyes glued to the screen. Then the scene ended for her as well. There was silence. She didn't know what to do, any more than I did.

Meanwhile, I was in the dark, literally, so I headed back upstairs. I had a feeling I had caught up with events, that the scene I had just witnessed was happening now. . . that Robin was somewhere nearby. She had to be in the house. She had to be. But where? I had searched everywhere. Or had I?

The GameBook beeped as I was walking up the stairs. "Well, it's about time." I said, and opened it. There was Robin, on the GameBook screen, saying, "I . . ."

Stauf stood before her. Tell him to get lost, Robin. But what would happen to her if she did that?

"Tell me what you want," Stauf said smoothly. "The world is waiting."

"Robin!" I yelled out, anguished. She couldn't buy into his crap! She couldn't ask for anything, not a single thing. Something terrible would happen to her if she did! I just knew it!

Robin looked around as though she heard me! "Carl?" she asked, wonderingly. "Carl? Where are you?"

"Never mind him!" Stauf snapped. "He's just an illusion. Tell me what you want." His voice was coaxing. "Your own show. . . Your own network?"

She paused, and looked at him long and hard. "My own network?" she asked, softly. He had pushed her button, all right. Power. Some people want money. Robin was the kind that wanted power, prestige, influence.

"Like that!" Henry Stauf snapped his fingers. "Is that what you want?"

I couldn't take this. "Robin!" I yelled out again. Would she hear me?

"Is it?" Stauf persisted, as though I hadn't said a word.

"I . . ."

"Say it!" he commanded, shouting right in her face. God, he was menacing.

I shouted again. "Don't!"

She faded from the GameBook.

There was the face of Samantha Ford staring back at me from the GameBook. What was she doing there, ready to talk to me? It was more than I could bear. I had to know what happened to Robin.

"She's gone." Samantha stated calmly.

I snarled, "Who are you?" even though I knew perfectly well who she was. I didn't want to feel grateful to anyone at this exact moment.

"Samantha. I'm the one who sent you the GameBook." She looked straight into my eyes. I felt my resentment melting. "I've been trying to help you save Robin." Her voice was tense.

I finally got to ask her the question I'd been wondering all along. "Samantha, why are you doing this?" I asked.

"I thought. . . hoped. . . you could defeat the house, but the house is too powerful. . . and we're all so weak. . . You've got to get out now."

Oh, right. Like I could just turn my back on Robin, after all I'd been through to get this far. I'd come here to rescue her from the house. I understood Samantha's reasoning. I, too, had felt that there was more to my presence here than just helping Robin.

After all, I certainly didn't want Robin back in my life on any romantic basis. But she was a person, a real person in real danger. And this house was evil. Maybe I could have had a hand in its destruction. I knew how powerful it was. I even understood the danger I was in. But—

"You know, I can't just leave her here," I told the woman in the GameBook.

In the distance, I heard Robin calling for me. She sounded frantic. She needed my help.

As I moved to go, Samantha warned, "Don't go! It's too late!"

"Samantha—" I didn't have time to argue with her. Robin was in real danger. That's just the way it was. "Look, I'll see you later, all right," I snapped, and closed the GameBook.

I had to find Robin before. . .

The GameBook beeped again. At least Samantha hadn't deserted me. *This eight letter word has "K-S-T" in the middle, in the beginning, and at the end.* Stauf sounded smug and triumphant. I wanted to kill him.

That's impossible. There must be a catch. What was it, though? I

realized how much I'd relied on Samantha's help all this time. I was really grateful she was still on my side.

"K-S-T" isn't in the beginning. "In" is. I wasn't following this. I needed to get to Robin. It was hard to concentrate.

"In" at the beginning, "K-S-T" in the middle and "and" at the end. If I lined all of those letters together. . .

Inkstand? *The word is "inkstand."* That was in the Library! I remembered having seen it on the desk.

I hurried to the Library. When I grasped the pen, it jumped out of the inkwell on its own and wrote on the paper: Play in my doll house!

This was a clue, wasn't it? I needed to return to the Doll Room. I'd seen the doll house in the Nursery.

I went down again through the floorboards in the Doll Room, and once I was in the Nursery I went over to the little doll house on the floor. The rooms looked like the rooms in this mansion. It was a little eerie.

I looked around the tiny house until I discovered what seemed to be a puzzle, tucked into the kitchen.

The tiles on the kitchen floor formed a grid. I turned to the GameBook for help, and found myself alone. Samantha said something about the connection getting weak.

I touched one of the tiles, found that I had little red stones. Of course, I thought, it's like Pente! The object is to get five stones in a row before Stauf does—or five captured pairs of two. I remembered that by surrounding a pair of the opponent's pieces from both ends, I could remove their pair from the board. I had played this game often as a younger man, when I was in college. Oh, Stauf was in for it now!

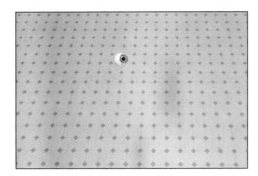 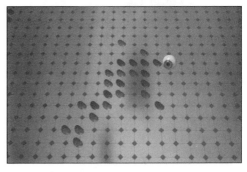

It was a tough game, and I had to keep my wits about me. My strategy of setting my pieces at every other space apart, to form triangles, helped. My ability to form open fours, that is, four in a row without one of his pieces closing either end of the row, defeated him in the end.

The board beckoned. I backed away from it, and went through the door to the Nursery. Once in the Nursery, I felt pulled toward the hallway and went along with my instinct. Ultimately, I found myself in Temple's bedroom.

All of a sudden, a brightly lit theater marquis filled the room. There was a cheering audience, or that's what I heard. I didn't see anyone. I thought I'd finally flipped my lid, only to realize that this was more of the house's insane magic. Let's Make A Real Deal, the marquis said. Henry Stauf, dressed in a tuxedo with a red bow tie, strode into the

room with me. He was smiling brightly and insincerely, the ultimate plastic grin of a game-show host. No doubt his true calling.

"Hello, Carl Denning, and welcome to LET'S MAKE A REAL DEAL!" He practically guffawed.

Was he thoroughly insane? What was his problem?

"Who the hell are you?" The question sounded rebellious, even to me. This whole situation felt totally out of control.

Stauf announced in a perfect game-show host voice, "Why, I'm Monty Stauf, your host on LET'S MAKE A REAL DEAL and have I got a real deal for you. . ." He looked down. "I wonder what this is in my pocket. . . ?"

He pulled out a wad of money. Was I crazy? Was this really happening? There was the roar of the invisible audience. I felt almost faint. Stauf went on, "Six, count 'em, six hundred dollars!"

So the deal was that he gave me six hundred dollars, in one hundred dollar bills. If I wanted to look behind a particular door—and yes, there were three of them, just like the TV show—I had to pay him $200.

It was completely surreal. The crowd sounds, the doors, the sight of Stauf playing game show host. It was sickening. I didn't know what to do. I wanted to turn and run, but I knew that wasn't possible. And what happened if I lost the game? Perhaps if I humor him, I thought, I can get out of this alive. I paid him $200.

"Thank you," responded Stauf. "Now which door?"

I chose the one in the middle. Where was all this leading? There was a big screen TV behind Door Number Two.

I paid him another two hundred. What was behind the other doors?

Door Number One opened to reveal Marie. She was dressed in lingerie, her generous cleavage, generously exposed. No doubt about it, she was a sexy woman. If woman was the right word. Monster, maybe.

"It's sweet Marie!" Stauf was saying in that announcer voice. "She can be yours, absolutely anytime, night or day!"

Marie squirmed pleasantly on her stool. "Anytime," she said, seductively.

"Imagine the hours of enjoyment, the fun you'll have with Marie! Much more exciting than watching TV!" Stauf

blathered. I'd rather be celibate my entire life, leaving matters in my own hands, so to speak, than tangle with Marie for even five minutes.

"You can watch me if you like," she purred. And smiled. It was creepy.

Suddenly, the TV came on and Samantha was in it. "Be strong, Carl. Don't give in to temptation," she warned. Geez! If she only knew how little Marie tempted me, after all I'd seen that girl—creature— do! Did Samantha think I was a total moron?

"Choose me." She said it calmly.

Stauf broke in, his voice loaded with scorn. "What a choice! Marie—sweet, sensuous, sexy Marie—or Samantha in a wheelchair! Hah!"

Samantha flushed. Stauf's derision had hit a nerve. Marie preened herself. The audience roared. Marie was sexy and sensuous, all right, and maybe under different circumstances I would have fallen under her spell. . . As I understood it, she was offering an eternity of sexual bliss. Hmm. . . I felt some stirring, some unnamed desire.

But where was Robin!?

"What's behind Door Number Three?" I asked Stauf. I had to pay him the last two hundred before he'd show me. As if the money meant anything to me. I made more than that in five minutes in front of the camera. And besides, Robin's life was at stake, and I was surrounded by the strange and insane forces of this house.

It was Robin. She was white-faced and on the verge of tears.

"Carl, I've been so frightened. Please, choose me. Save me." I was just about to go toward her when she said, "I . . . love you."

That stopped me dead in my tracks. She didn't sound like Robin at all! And it was exactly what I had imagined she'd say, oh so long ago,

when I was riding through the Connecticut countryside on my mission of knight errantry. I felt a tug at my heart.

Marie broke in, "I'll give you anything you want. Anything and everything." She writhed around on her chair like a cat in heat. She sure was sexy. . . I felt her allure surround me.

"Don't listen to them, Carl. You'll be lost forever." The urgency in Samantha's voice brought me back to the present.

Stauf tried to shut Samantha up, but she persisted, "He's afraid of you, Carl. Choose me. Destroy the power of this hellish house."

What was I going to do?

Robin spoke again. "Carl, you have to choose me. After all we've been through. . ." Her eyes were dark, luminous. I found it difficult to look straight into them. Then she said the other words I thought I'd wanted to hear her say, ever since she broke up with me: "I need you."

I struggled with the conflicting forces in my mind. Behind Door Number One was Marie, who exuded sexuality, desire, lust. It was a powerful intoxicant. A promise of ecstacy to come. Desire incarnate!

Then, behind Door Number Two sat Samantha. Brave. Loyal. Strong. She had helped me, but was that reason enough to choose her? We were both trying to save Robin, weren't we? But could I just abandon her now?

Then there was Robin. She was saying the words I had longed to hear. I had come to rescue her, and I was now in a position to do so. But things had changed. This house had changed me, and her as well. I found myself asking if I really cared anymore. Perhaps she wasn't the most important thing in my life now. Sure, she was my. . . friend? Lover? Well, she was my producer, after all. Had she given in to Stauf or not? Just how trustworthy was she? In the end, did I love her? Did I care?

Marie was vamping. "Anytime. . . anyplace. . . any way. . . you want me."

Stauf looked me in the eye. He was demented. Inhuman!

"Well, what'll it be, sport? The choice is yours . . ."

It certainly was. I knew I had until the stroke of midnight to make my decision. After that? I made my decision, shaking off all confusion. As I stepped forward to the door, I felt a surge of confidence in myself. I had navigated my way through this awful mansion and its twisted, evil, brain-bending puzzles—and defeated it through my own quick thinking and the help of the GameBook. And now it was over. I knew exactly what I had to do.

As I opened the door which led to the woman of my choice and looked into her eyes, I felt a surge of strength run through my body. I was strong, stronger and more powerful even than this house and its evil! I was still alive, and I had triumphed!

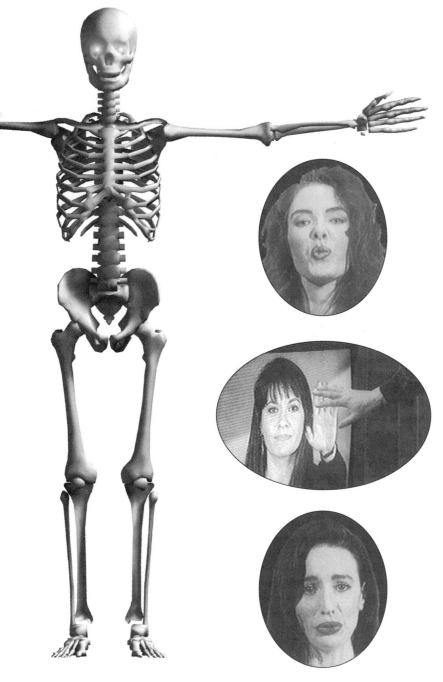

THE 11ᵀᴴ HOUR

THE SCRIPT

11TH Hour

Script by Matthew Costello

Revisions by David Wheeler
final draft
April 15, 1993

IMPORTANT NOTE

This is the original, uncut script for *The 11th Hour*. Notice that it was last revised in 1993. This script contains suggested scenes for both PG- and R-rated versions.

There is not, never was, and will not be an R-rated version of *The 11th Hour*.

These suggested scenes were never created. We've left them in the script for historical accuracy and for your interest only. Again, there is only *one* version of *The 11th Hour*—the one you have! That's it.

INTRODUCTION

INTRO-1 INT / DENNING'S COUNTRY HOME - AFTERNOON

CARL DENNING is watching television.
His handsome face is grim and determined, bathed in the flickering light of the TV's images.
On the TV screen an anchorwoman is reading the evening news.

ANCHOR

State Police have called off the intense search for producer Robin Morales
of television's *Case Unsolved.*

She continues to speak in voice-over as the screen is filled with an image of an intelligent
looking woman with compelling beauty. The words "ROBIN MORALES—CASE
UNSOLVED PRODUCER" are superimposed across the bottom of the screen.

ANCHOR (V/O)

Morales was researching a story about the famed haunted house in the small town of Harley-
on-Hudson—the abandoned mansion of Henry Stauf.

The anchorperson continues to talk over images of old newspaper stories from the 1920's
and mysterious photos of HENRY STAUF and his ill-fated guests. The screen switches to
current images of the main street of Harley-on-Hudson

ANCHOR (V/O)

Police have expressed concern that Morales' disappearance may be connected to a series of
killings that have plagued the Hudson Valley this year.

Another IMAGE, a BODY, lying in the grass. Signs of violence, blood, the skin discolored,
leaves and twigs stuck to the body.

ANCHOR (V/O)
So far, four women and three men have been victims fitting a pattern of homicide,
and several others are missing.

Another image of Robin comes onto the screen.

ANCHOR (V/O CONT'D)
Robin Morales has been missing for more than three weeks and seems to have vanished
without a trace.

The anchorwoman again appears on the screen.

ANCHOR
She is the producer for the very popular and flamboyant *Case Unsolved*
reporter Carl Denning.

An image of Denning fills the screen, smiling, confident.

ANCHOR (V/O)
Denning is said to have been in seclusion in his country home in Connecticut since Morales'
disappearance. It's rumored that the two were romantically involved before....

*Denning clicks off the TV with a remote switch. He slumps back in his chair and massages
his temples. He looks up at the sound of a doorbell ringing, gets out of his chair and crosses
the room and opens the door. A UPS truck is pulling away and a package is on the doorstep.*

*Denning crouches down and picks it up and goes back inside. He returns to his chair and
opens the package, revealing a small, portable computer of some kind.*

*He switches it on, and a game flickers to life on the machine... "Funhouse From Hell" -
Cartoony images of mayhem, monsters... Slowly, the computer game changes to an image of
Robin looking frightened in the basement of an old house.
She speaks to him from the small screen.*

ROBIN
Carl... help me... please!... I can't get out... I....

*The image of Robin fades away and the videoscreen goes blank as if the game
has shut itself off. Denning shakes the box and clicks it on and off but it seems to have died.*

DENNING
What is this?

*He sets the game computer on the arm of the chair, gets to his feet and begins to pace. The
game starts beeping. He grabs it and switches it on. An image of the Stauf mansion appears
briefly and fades away and the game shuts down again.*

DENNING
Damn!

*Then the screen comes alive for another brief moment: An image of Robin appears. She
mouths the word "Help" but there is no sound and the picture quickly fades.
Denning pulls on a leather windbreaker and stuffs the game in his pocket as he crosses the
room and leaves in a rush.*

INTRO-2 EXT/DENNING'S COUNTRY HOUSE IN CONNECTICUT - DAY

Denning pulls on a dark-shielded helmet and straddles a high-tech motorcycle. The engine growls to life and he guns the throttle and peels out of the driveway in a spray of gravel.

Title Card:

THE 11TH HOUR

Followed by the credits

INTRO-3 EXT/TWO LANE COUNTRY HIGHWAY

The speeding bike cuts a screaming shock wave through the quiet forest.

Denning rides with precise concentration and skill and though he's hidden behind the dark visor, his thoughts are almost visible... Robin.

INTRO-4 INT/ESPRESSO BAR - DAY - [FLASHBACK]

Denning and Robin are sitting across from each other at a small table in a New York espresso bar. They are looking at each other with playful eyes, not speaking, holding each other's gaze. Finaly, Robin breaks the silence.

ROBIN
What?

He smiles and shakes his head.

DENNING
I have a rule about people I work with.

She laughs softly.

ROBIN
Oh?

DENNING
Yeah, I... uh... I don't get involved.

ROBIN
Uh-huh... I have the same rule.

There is another silence and they continue to hold each other's gaze.

ROBIN (CONT'D)
It's a good rule.

DENNING
Yeah... Yeah it sure is.

ROBIN
Keeps everything on a professional level.

DENNING
It does... It works for me.

ROBIN
Yes... me too.

DENNING
So... uh... I'm kinda thinking about breaking this rule.

She smiles.

ROBIN
So am I.

INTRO-5 EXT/HIGHWAY - DAY

The high-tech engine continues to shriek in the quiet forest.

INTRO-6 INT / DENNING'S CAR - [FLASHBACK]

Robin and Denning are making frantic love in the front seat of a car. He is in the driver's seat with the back tilted so that it's almost flat. She is straddling him, her skirt hiked up. It appears as though they are parked in a torrential downpour but the flood of water rapidly decreases and suddenly she scrambles back into her seat and they are hurriedly re-arranging their clothes and laughing as the car rolls out of a car wash, greeted by a confused-looking attendant.

INTRO-6-PG INT / DENNING'S CAR - [FLASHBACK] [pgversion]

Robin and Denning appear to be parked in a torrential downpour. They're sitting in the front seat, leaned together in an embrace. The flood of water rapidly decreases and suddenly they are laughing and hurriedly trying to look as if nothing were happening as the car rolls out of a car wash, greeted by a confused-looking attendant.

INTRO-7 EXT/HIGHWAY - DAY

Denning continues his high-speed journey through the countryside.

INTRO-8 INT/ESPRESSO BAR - DAY [FLASHBACK]

*Denning and Robin are again sitting at their favorite table in the espresso bar. She looks
upset and he is obviously angry, though he tries to cover it with a nonchalant attitude.*

DENNING
I thought you liked me.

She is on the verge of crying.

ROBIN
You know I do.

DENNING
Didn't I even hear the word "love" whispered occasionally?

She closes her eyes as a tear rolls down her cheek.

ROBIN
I just can't go on like this. People... everyone thinks I got to be your producer
by sleeping with you.

He looks at her a moment then shrugs.

DENNING
So...didn't you?

ROBIN
How can you say that? You of all people...

You know I'm a good producer.

He speaks in a cold voice.

DENNING
You're good at a lot of things, Robin.

ROBIN
Carl, I'm sorry...

DENNING
Who's next? A network president.

His comment sobers her and she looks at him a moment before responding.

ROBIN
I'll ignore that.

DENNING
Don't. It was from the heart.

ROBIN
Why can't you be more understanding?

DENNING
Yeah, right.

He pushes back from the table and stands.

DENNING (CONT'D)
I guess I'll see you in the office on Monday, Ms. Morales.

ROBIN
No... I'll be in Harley-on-Hudson next week.

DENNING
Oh? I thought that story gave you the creeps.

ROBIN
I just need to get away for a while.

DENNING
Oh, I see... get away from the creeps.

ROBIN
Carl...

DENNING
Well maybe I'll get lucky and you'll become another missing person in Harley.

ROBIN
Don't say that. It scares me.

He shrugs.

DENNING
I already did.

He turns and leaves.

INTRO-9 EXT / DOWNTOWN HARLEY - NIGHT

Denning's built-for-speed bike motors slowly along Main Street in downtown Harley-on-Hudson.

INTRO-10 EXT / AT THE GATE - NIGHT

The motorcycle turns onto an overgrown driveway and comes to a stop at an old, rusted, iron gate. Denning dismounts, gets a flashlight from a compartment on the bike and switches it on.

Denning pushes against the black metal gate, and it creaks open, scraping against the concrete underfoot. The top of the gate looks dangerous, with sharp, jagged spikes.

INTRO-11 EXT/MANSION - NIGHT

Denning crosses a field, overgrown with weeds , approaching a huge, dark Victorian home —THE STAUF MANSION. The building is a black shape, barely outlined by grayish clouds and the dull glow of a waning moon masked by the clouds.

INTRO-12 EXT/MANSION PORCH - NIGHT

Flashlight in hand, Denning moves up the front steps to the door. He tries the handle but it's rusted closed. He pushes the door but it doesn't move. He rams the door with his shoulder. Nothing. He steps back.

DENNING
Damn!

There is a muffled electronic beeping noise. He reaches into his pocket and takes out the computer gamebook. There is an image on the screen: the number "3." Denning looks perplexed. The computer continues to beep in bursts of three. Beep beep beep. Denning approaches the door again. He doesn't seem to have a whole lot of faith in the gesture but he knocks on the door. Three times. And the door opens, much to his surprise. He looks at the little computer, impressed.

DENNING
Well all right!

He looks into the doorway. It's black inside. Denning shrugs and goes into the darkness. The door slams shut behind him.

... And the game begins...

MODULE I SCENES—HARLEY-ON-HUDSON

I-1 EXT/COFFEE SHOP ON MAIN STREET - DAY

There is a line of pick-up trucks parked outside a coffee shop in "downtown" Harley. Like the rest of the town, the coffee shop seems frozen in time—somewhere in the late fifties when the freeway went in and traffic (and life in general) began to pass Harley by. Like a flash to the present, a convertible driven by a young, beautiful woman in dark glasses, motors down Main Street and pulls into a parking spot between two beat up pick-ups in front of the coffee shop.
The coffee shop is filled with breakfast customers and all eyes are on the convertible. The woman gets out and she's dressed in a fashionable short skirt, heels and a tailored jacket—all in black—looking as if she'd be more at home in a Manhattan design studio than the sleepy town of Harley. It's Robin. She walks up to the front door of the coffee shop and goes in.

I-2 INT/COFFEE SHOP - DAY

Robin enters the coffee shop and stands just inside the door next to the cash register, keeping her dark glasses on. All motion has come to a complete stop and everyone is looking at her. Finally a waitress speaks up. She's a truck-stop woman—kind of voluptuous, a little rough edged and attractive in an earthy sort of way. She has a prosthetic hand protruding from the sleeve of her sweater. Her name is Eileen Wiley.

EILEEN
Just sit anywhere, honey. Menu's are on the table.

ROBIN
Thanks. Is there a non-smoking section?

There is a slight rumble of laughter. Virtually everyone including the cook is smoking. Eileen grins and shakes her head. Robin walks towards a booth by the window. The only sound is the clicking of her heels and the slight rustle of her clothing. She sits down, takes off her dark glasses and inspects the menu. Slowly, everyone goes back to their business and the sound level raises back up to that of a normal coffee shop environment. Eileen comes over to Robin's table.

EILEEN
What can I get for you this morning?

ROBIN
Do you have oat-bran muffins?

EILEEN
This isn't an oat-bran kind of place, honey. We're big on chocolate donuts here.

ROBIN
I don't suppose you have any Perrier water.

EILEEN
Let me check... Hey Slim, we got any Perrier?

Slim is the cook. He sticks his head out from the kitchen.

SLIM
Fresh out of Perrier, Eileen. Had a big run on it this morning.

Everyone in the restaurant laughs.

EILEEN
Sorry, honey. How about a San Pelegrino?

ROBIN
Oh? That would be fine.

EILEEN
I'm kidding, hon. The only water we got comes out of the tap.

ROBIN
Just bring me a donut and a coffee.

EILEEN
Now you're talkin'. Shall I make that a capuccino?

ROBIN
Enough with the jokes, okay?

EILEEN
No, I'm serious. As unlikely as it seems, we actually have an espresso machine.

Robin smiles and shrugs.

ROBIN
Okay.

EILEEN
Be right back.

She leaves and Robin takes out a small palm-size computer and begins to type.

FADE TO:
Master Object:

I-3 INT / COFFEESHOP - DAY

Eileen returns with the donut.

EILEEN
Here you go. Be right back with the coffee.

ROBIN
You're Eileen Wiley, aren't you?

EILEEN
Who wants to know?

ROBIN
I'm Robin Morales. I'm a producer with *Case Unsolved*—the TV show.

EILEEN
Is that the one with Carl Denning?

ROBIN
Uh-huh.

EILEEN
Ooh I like him...Wouldn't mind serving him up a couple of specials.

She laughs and Robin smiles.

EILEEN (CONT'D)
What's he like?

ROBIN
He's...uh...he's a man.

EILEEN
You mean he's a man like you can't live with him or a man like you can't live without him?

Robin thinks about it a moment then grins.

ROBIN
He's both.

EILEEN
Aren't they all?

They both laugh and Eileen sits down.

EILEEN (CONT'D)
So what are you doing in Harley?

ROBIN
I'm researching a story on the Stauf Mansion.

Eileen's mood changes in an instant.

EILEEN
I can't help you.

ROBIN
You're the only person who's survived an encounter with the mansion.

EILEEN
Who told you that?

ROBIN
Everyone else has either disappeared or died.

EILEEN
It's all just stories.

ROBIN
What happened to you there?

EILEEN
You know so much already, why do you need me to tell you.

ROBIN
The newspaper said a guard dog tore your hand off. What really happened?

Eileen's eyes are flooded with tears. She gets up out of the booth.

EILEEN
I gotta get back to work.

ROBIN
I'm sorry I upset you.

Eileen tries to laugh it off.

EILEEN
Not me. Be right back with that coffee.

She leaves.

Robin glances around the restaurant. Once again everyone is looking at her...But now there is a touch of anger in their eyes. Robin puts on her dark glasses as if to hide behind them and looks out the window.

I-4 INT/MOTEL OFFICE - DAY

A desk clerk is struggling with a crossword puzzle in the office of THE HARLEY INN, a dingy, run down, 1950's motel. He looks up as the door opens and smiles leeringly.

CLERK
Hello, Marie.

An eighteen year old girl moves with a slow sensual saunter towards the desk. She has a look of petulant sexuality, dressed in a short denim skirt, white high heels and a white T-sirt.

MARIE
Where's Chuck?

CLERK
I thought maybe you were here to see me.

MARIE
You wish... Is he in his office?

The clerk checks his watch.

CLERK
He's got a meeting in five minutes. He hasn't got time for you today, Marie.

She smirks.

MARIE
Just tell 'im I'm here.

He picks up the telephone and punches a button.

CLERK
Chuck, Marie Wiley's here to see you... But you got a meeting at eight... Okay, okay.

He hangs up and reaches behind him for a room key and hands it to Marie.

CLERK

Lucky number 7... Have fun.

She takes the key and turns and leaves without another word. The clerk watches Marie's hips move under her tight fitting, skirt as she goes out the door.

I-5 EXT/HARLEY INN - DAY

Chuck Lynch hurries past a line of motel-room doors. He's middle aged, dressed in a cheap suit and kind of handsome in a sleazy sort of way. He stops in front of room number seven, unlocks it with a master key, checks to see if anyone's looking and goes in.

I-6 INT/A ROOM AT THE HARLEY INN - DAY

Chuck quickly closes the door behind him and begins to loosen his tie. Marie is standing by the window across the room on the other side of the bed.

CHUCK

I've only got a few minutes.

He leaves the knot in the tie pulls the loop over his head and hangs it on the doorknob. He fumbles with the buttons of his shirt. Marie just stands by the window playing with the control rod of the mini-blind, opening and closing the slats. Chuck pulls his shirt off, tosses it on a chair and reaches to untie a shoe.

CHUCK

C'mon, Marie. We gotta hurry. Let's get in bed.

She just looks at him. Playing with the wand, the continually changing slatted pattern of light playing across her face.

CHUCK (CONT'D)

Something wrong?

MARIE

Maybe I'm not in the mood for a quickie, Chuck. That's something you can do with your wife.

He crosses the room, shirtless, with one shoe on. She turns and looks out the window.

He wraps his arms around her from behind and holds her close, pressing his face into her hair.

CHUCK

C'mon, sweet Marie. Chucky can do a lot in a few short minutes... Make those minutes seem like hours.

He kisses her neck and she begins to respond, closing her eyes and moving slowly, sensuously against him. He caresses her hips then pulls the front of her T-shirt up over her breasts. She turns in his arms and presses her bare skin against his chest. They begin to kiss with a passionate hunger. She licks his ear then bites him on the side of his neck. Hard. He inhales sharply. Harder.

CHUCK
OW!

She draws blood and he pulls back, clutching his neck.

CHUCK (CONT'D)
Jeeze, Marie! What're you doing?

She just laughs. He looks at the blood on his fingertips.

CHUCK
How'm I gonna hide this from my wife? If you're gonna bite me, do it
where it doesn't show.

MARIE
Time's up, Chuck.

She slowly pulls her shirt down, covering herself. He checks his watch.

CHUCK
Damn!

He rapidly crosses the room, pulls on his shirt and buttons the collar.

*He checks himself in the mirror and the bite mark shows no matter how high he
pulls the collar up.*

CHUCK
How'm I gonna go to this meeting with a fresh bite mark on my neck?

She sits on the edge of the bed.

MARIE
Don't go.

CHUCK

Oh, yeah. Sure. I can't afford to miss this. I got a business to run. It's about money!

MARIE

You can do whatever you want, Chuck.

She lays back on the bed and lightly caresses her thighs. He stares at her, mesmerized. She slowly pushes the hem of her skirt up. Chuck inhales deeply. She arches up slightly and slides the skirt up over her panty covered hips. She looks at him, her eyes clouded with passion.

MARIE

You leaving, Chuck?

CHUCK

Oh baby...

He tears his shirt off and fumbles with his belt buckle. She laughs, her eyes now filled with delight...and a touch of evil.

I-6-PG INT/A ROOM AT THE HARLEY INN - DAY. [PG VERSION]

Chuck quickly closes the door behind him and begins to loosen his tie.

Marie is standing by the window across the room on the other side of the bed.

CHUCK

I've only got a few minutes.

Marie just stands by the window playing with the control rod of the mini-blind, opening and closing the slats. Chuck pulls his shirt off, tosses it on a chair and reaches to untie a shoe. She just looks at him. Playing with the wand, the continually changing slatted pattern of light playing across her face.

CHUCK (CONT'D)

Something wrong?

MARIE

I don't like it when you don't have time for me.

He crosses the room, shirtless, hobbling with one shoe on. She turns and looks out the window. He wraps his arms around her from behind and holds her close, pressing his face into her hair. He kisses her neck. She turns in his arms, kisses him then bites him on the side of his neck. Hard.

CHUCK

OW!

She draws blood and he pulls back, clutching his neck.

CHUCK (CONT'D)

Jeeze, Marie! What're you doing?

She just laughs. He looks at the blood on his fingertips.

MARIE
Time's up, Chuck.

He checks his watch.

CHUCK
Damn!

He rapidly crosses the room, pulls on his shirt and buttons the collar. He checks himself in the mirror and the bite mark shows no matter how high he pulls the collar up.

CHUCK
How'm I gonna go to this meeting with a fresh bite mark on my neck?

She sits on the edge of the bed.

MARIE
Don't go.

CHUCK
Oh, yeah. Sure. I can't afford to miss this. I got a business to run. It's about money!

MARIE
You can do whatever you want, Chuck.

She lays back on the bed and gives him a vixenish look. He stares at her, mesmerized.

MARIE
You leaving, Chuck?

CHUCK
Oh baby...

He bends to take off his other shoe as he hops towards the bed. She laughs, her eyes filled with delight...and a touch of evil.

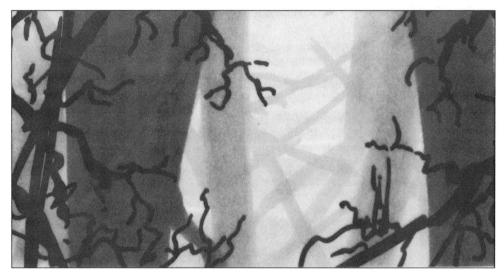

I-7 EXT/A WOODED AREA - DAY

Black high heels step carefully through the bramble. The heels slip and wobble and sometimes stick in the soft ground. Legs in nylon stockings which catch on the brush. Moving, pressing on until coming to a stop next to some rocks. The knees bend and Robin crouches down into view, carefully examining the rocks. The rocks are stained red. She reaches out and touches the stain with her finger tips. Some of the stain comes off onto her fingers and she rubs at it with her thumb. There is a man's voice behind her.

VOICE
Yeah, it's blood.

Robin whirls around to see a uniformed policeman—Harley police chief Jim Martin. He blocks the morning sun, a dark figure, a shadow man.

ROBIN
I was just...

MARTIN
I know what you're doing. You were looking for the scene of a crime—and you found it. You did good...for a TV person. I'm impressed.

Robin smiles.

ROBIN
I'm Robin Morales.

She extends her hand and Martin takes it.

MARTIN
Jim Martin. Chief of the Harley Police.

Robin raises an eyebrow.

ROBIN

Chief! Now I'm impressed.

MARTIN

Yeah, well there's only me and one other guy and he's the co-chief and that's pretty well the whole damn force.

Robin laughs.

MARTIN (CONT'D)

So what're you doin' out here lookin' at blood on the rocks, Robin?

ROBIN

I'm researching a story. I work for...

MARTIN

I know, I know. Case Unsolved. Word travels fast in a small town...But I understood you were doin a story 'bout the haunted house.

ROBIN

I am...But I think there's a connection. I mean all the stories of death and disappearance surrounding the house must be related to this current rash of crime. Isn't it more of the same? Don't you think they might be related?

MARTIN

No, I don't.

ROBIN

Why not?

MARTIN

Because the haunted house is a ghost story and I don't believe in ghosts. But this is the real thing. This is MURDER, Robin. It was no ghost that spilled that blood. And whoever did it hasn't been caught, so I don't think you should be out wanderin' around in the woods by yourself.

ROBIN

I can take care of myself.

MARTIN

That may be...But you're running an unnecessary risk...Stick to the ghost story.

ROBIN

What do you think happened to Eileen Wiley's hand?

MARTIN

Got bit off by a dog.

ROBIN

Do you really believe that?

MARTIN
Sure I do.

ROBIN
Well I don't. I mean, how could a dog do that?

Martin shrugs.

MARTIN
Probably one of those damned Rotweillers or something.

ROBIN
Oh, come on chief. Were there other bite marks on her? Did anyone find the dog? Did anyone find the hand?

MARTIN
I don't know. It was before my time. You'd have to ask Doc Thorton. He's the one sewed her up.

ROBIN
Is he still around?

MARTIN
Barely. Doc's gettin up there, but he's still breathin'. Come on, I'll drive you by his office. You can follow me in that snazzy little car.

ROBIN
Thanks, Chief, that's very kind of you.

They begin to leave the scene of the crime.

MARTIN
Call me Jim, will you? Kind've embarrassing to be called chief when there's nobody to be chief over.

ROBIN
Okay, Jim.

MARTIN
You know, you're not exactly dressed for trompin' around in the woods. You should get some boots. Maybe they make a special "TV Producer" designer hiking boot...

She laughs and they disappear into the woods. A soft breath of wind causes the leaves to shimmer and brings with it a sound of beautiful, ethereal music. Then, over the music, there is another sound. A digging noise, as if in the distance but—as it grows louder—it reveals itself as coming from the ground. Under the blood stained rocks. The sound of earth moving is joined by a new noise, a low, distorted grunting. The red stains on the rocks deepen, then glisten as if fresh. There's movement on the ground. The wind gusts and blows away the top covering of leaves. The rocks starts to ooze blood. They pulsate, as if alive. And from the earth floor, there are things pressing up, indistinguishable at first, but then—

The definite impression of , a man, a woman, a child, others, all trying to break through the surface of the earth. Until, like a balloon, it all explodes, and in slow motion the dirt and leaves, and screaming faces go rushing by—leaving an empty black hole. The hole seems bottomless but there is something glimmering, a pinpoint of light, rushing from the bottom of the hole, rushing closer, until there's another face—the face of HENRY STAUF, tinted red, dripping blood, laughing...louder...the STAUF head begins to bulge, transforming—and for the first time there is a glimpse of the master behind the puppets. Sunken, reptilian eyes, an ancient mouth with teeth. Devouring everything into its blackness.

FADE UP

I-8 INT / THE STAUF HOUSE - DAY

[Trigger: Clicking on a painting of the basement which is on the wall of any room Denning is in—after all other scenes have been witnessed.] Liquid fills the painted catacomb, drowning the sepulchres. Until the basement appears as a still, shimmering lake. Robin is crouched on the steps, above the shimmering pool.

ROBIN
Oh, God—help. Please help.

I-9 INT/STAUF HOUSE HALLWAY - DAY

The beeper on Denning's game book goes off. He pulls it out of his jacket and switches it on. The view of Robin in the basement appears on the screen. Denning watches as a skeleton hand snakes up out of the pool, reaching for her leg.

DENNING
Robin! Move! Get up—get—
Robin looks around as if she can hear him.

ROBIN
Carl?

The HAND is about to close around her—

DENNING
Look out!

—and the image fades.

FADE TO BLACK

...END OF MODULE I

MODULE II SCENES—MYSTERIOUS CHARACTERS

These first scenes become active after solving the Master Puzzle...after all the Module One scenes have been viewed.

II-1 INT/SAMANTHA FORD'S ART STUDIO - DAY

FADE UP on a video monitor which contains the scene of Robin in the basement. Robin scurries up a couple of steps and the skeleton hand sinks back into the pool. The monitor is being watched by Samantha Ford. She is an attractive woman whose intelligence is so powerful it's almost palpable. The picture begins to fade on the monitor and Samantha begins typing on the keyboard with furious speed. The picture goes blank.

SAMANTHA
Damn!

II-2 INT/STAUF HAUS HALLWAY - DAY

DENNING
Damn!

The screen on his gamebook is blank. He clicks it on and off and pushes a few buttons...but nothing happens.

II-3 INT/SAMANTHA'S STUDIO - DAY

Samantha pushes back from the monitor. She's in a wheelchair. She wheels around to another monitor and keyboard and begins to type. The monitor comes to life with a view of the Stauf Mansion. She positions the cursor at the entry and clicks on the door. The monitor now shows the inside foyer and the picture begins to track down the hallway, searching.

SAMANTHA
Where are you, Denning?

II-4 EXT/DR. THORTON'S OFFICE - DAY

Robin brings her convertible to a stop behind Martin's police cruiser in front of a charming country house with a picket fence. They both get out of their cars.

MARTIN
Well, here it is...Doc Thorton's.

ROBIN
Thanks for your help.

MARTIN
No problem. Good luck.

ROBIN
Okay, see you.

MARTIN
You take care.

She pauses and looks at him. An attraction between them is simmering.

ROBIN
I will.

He smiles and she turns towards the doctor's house.

He watches her walk through the picket gate, along the path and up the stairs to the porch. She turns and glances back before going inside. He gets in his cruiser and drives away.

II-5 INT/DR. THORTON'S OFFICE - WAITING ROOM - DAY

There's a young woman sitting behind a desk in a reception area. Robin comes in through the door and approaches the desk. The woman at the desk is Marie Wiley. She looks up from a magazine when Robin reaches the desk. She seems bored and put out.

MARIE
Can I help you?

ROBIN
I'd like to see Dr, Thorton if he's available.

MARIE
He's available. Are you a patient of his?

ROBIN
No, I...

Marie tosses a clipboard with a form attached in Robin's direction.

MARIE
Fill this out.

ROBIN
Actually I'm not here as a patient. I'm a producer for *Case Unsolved*—the television show?
—and I'd like to interview him.

MARIE
You're kidding.

ROBIN
No.

MARIE
What do ya wanna interview him for?

ROBIN
I need to discuss that with Dr. Thorton.

Marie shrugs and presses a button on an intercom.

MARIE
Hey, Doc. You awake?

The doctor can be heard clearing his throat.

THORTON (OS)
Yes...Of course.

MARIE
There's someone here from a TV show. Says she wants to interview you.

THORTON
Well, send her in, Marie.

Marie cocks her head towards a door and Robin moves in that direction.

ROBIN
Thanks.

MARIE
Sure.

She goes back to her magazine as Robin goes in through the door.

II-6 INT/THORTON'S OFFICE - DAY

Robin enters Dr. Thorton's office and crosses to his desk with her hand extended.

ROBIN
Hello, Dr. Thorton. Robin Morales. I'm a producer with *Case Unsolved*.

He rises to shake her hand then sits back down behind his desk. Robin sits across from him.

THORTON
What can I do for you, Robin?

ROBIN
I'm researching a story on the Stauf Mansion.

He looks interested.

THORTON
Oh?

ROBIN
I'm trying to follow a story line involving Eileen Wiley. The legend...or myth or...
story...seems to be that she's the only one to have survived an encounter with the mansion.
Everyone else has either died or disappeared.

Thorton chuckles.

THORTON
There are a lot of stories about that old house.

ROBIN
I've been told that you treated her the night she lost her hand.

THORTON
Well...Yes...That's true. I did.

ROBIN
What do you think happened to her hand?

THORTON
It got bitten off by a dog. Everybody knows that.

ROBIN
So I've heard. But did it really look to you like a dog did it?

THORTON
I don't know. I've never seen a hand bitten off by a dog before. Never even heard of such a
thing. Eileen's kinda unique that way. She's a bit of a celebrity around these parts because of it.

ROBIN
But really, doctor, what did it look like to you?

He pauses a moment.

THORTON
Robin, it was a mess. A bloody mess

II-7 INT / THORTON'S OFFICE - NIGHT [FLASHBACK]

Thorton is bent over a patient on his examining table, her screams fill the room.
Then—unexpectedly—the wounded arm, bloody and terrifying, shoots up.

II-8 INT/THORTON'S OFFICE - DAY

ROBIN
I just think there's more to this Eileen Wiley thing than meets the eye.

II-9 INT/THORTON'S WAITING ROOM - DAY

Marie has the intercom swithched on and is listening to every word with great intensity.

II-10 INT/THORTON'S OFFICE - DAY

THORTON
Have you talked to Eileen?

ROBIN
I've tried, but I didn't get very far.

THORTON
It was a traumatic time for her.
Robin nods and sighs.

ROBIN
I know...And I hate to bring it back to her...It's just that she's the only one who's had an experience at the mansion and lived to tell about it.

THORTON
Not the only one.

ROBIN
What do you mean?

THORTON
Samantha Ford.

ROBIN
Who's she?

THORTON
The one nobody talks about...She was there that night with Eileen. The two of them sneaked onto the grounds and broke into the house together.

ROBIN
Why isn't she mentioned in any of the articles?

THORTON
Samantha's family had a lot of influence and were able to keep her out of it...But if you think Eileen's hand is a mystery, well...Samantha has been paralyzed from the waist down and confined to a wheelchair ever since that night!

II-11 INT/STAUF HAUSE - NIGHT

Denning looks down a hallway in the house.

A ghostly image comes running towards him. It's a young Eileen Wiley, still a teenager. She runs up to Denning and stops, looking terrified.

EILEEN
Something's happened to Samantha...Something's got her.

DENNING
I...uh...Who's Samantha?

EILEEN
Can you help her?

DENNING
I...I don't know.

Eileen looks like she's about to crumble.

EILEEN
I have to get out of here...I'm scared!

She turns and runs.

DENNING
Wait! Where's Robin?

Her ghostly image fades into the darkness.

II-12 EXT/SAVAGE RAPIDS DAM - DAY

Chuck is pressed up against Marie, her back against the railing as rushing water cascades over the dam below them. Her skirt is pushed up revealing stockings and garter belt and Chuck is caressing the bare skin above the stocking tops.   They are kissing passionately. Suddenly Chuck freezes. Marie has brought a straight razor up to his throat. She looks at him intensely with menace in her eyes. Chuck is terrified. Her face takes on a devilish grin as she folds the razor and puts it in Chuck's pocket. Her eyes are now filled with playful delight. She pulls him close and they are back at it, kissing with a fierce hunger.

II-12-PG EXT/SAVAGE RAPIDS DAM - DAY [PG VERSION]

Chuck is kissing Marie, her back against the railing as rushing water cascades over the dam below them. Suddenly Chuck freezes. Marie has brought a straight razor up to his throat. She looks at him intensely with menace in her eyes. Chuck is terrified. Her face takes on a devilish grin as she folds the razor and puts it in Chuck's pocket. Her eyes are now filled with playful delight as she pulls him close again.

II-13 INT/COFFEE SHOP - NIGHT

Eileen is getting ready to close the coffee shop when Marie comes in.

EILEEN
Hi, honey. Want something to eat?

Marie sits at the counter.

MARIE
Just coffee.

Eileen pours a cup for Marie and one for herself.

EILEEN
How's work?

MARIE
Boring. Got any cigarettes?

Eileen picks up a pack from behind the counter.

EILEEN
You know I don't like you smoking.

Marie takes a cigarette and lights it with a lighter from her pocket and offers up a light for Eileen.

MARIE
Yeah, well...like mother like daughter.

Eileen takes a drag and exhales a cloud of smoke.

EILEEN
I guess there's no one to blame but myself.

Marie takes a deep drag on her cigarette, exhales the smoke and smiles.

MARIE
I guess.

EILEEN
Marie, I...I hear you've been seeing Chuck Lynch.

MARIE
So?

EILEEN
He's a married man.

MARIE
So who cares?

EILEEN
So I care. You'll get a reputation, Marie. I don't want people calling my daughter a tramp.

MARIE
Yeah, well, like I said...Like mother like daughter.

EILEEN
Marie!

MARIE
Save it.

Marie gets off the stool and heads for the door.

EILEEN
Marie!

Marie stops and turns and gives her mother a menacing look,

MARIE
What?

Eileen is taken aback by Marie's forcefulness.

EILEEN
I...uh...will you be home tonight?

Marie shrugs.

MARIE
Maybe.

She turns and walks out the door. Eileen watches her go then shakes her head and angrily stubs out her cigarette.

II-14 EXT/SAVAGE RAPIDS DAM - NIGHT

Robin is walking along the concrete abutment next to the dam. The water crashes over the dam with an ominous roar. She stops and looks behind her as if someone were following her. She sees no one. She walks on a little faster. The roar of the river seems to increase. She begins to run.

II-15 EXT/HARLEY INN - NIGHT

Robin arrives at the motel out of breath. It looks deserted. She hurries along the dark corridor towards her room. She looks over her shoulder and, while her head is turned, a man steps out of the darkness and catches her in his arms... It's Chief Martin.

MARTIN
Better watch where you're going there, Robin.

Robin looks breathless and terrified.

MARTIN
You okay?

ROBIN
I...I just...

She's having trouble catching her breath.

He looks at her, waiting.

ROBIN
I'm sorry, I was...I don't know what I was doing.

He grins.

MARTIN
Whatever it was, you were moving with impressive speed.

She manages a smile, then laughs at herself.

ROBIN
I guess I was.

MARTIN
I got something for you.

He steps over to his police Explorer, reaches inside and returns with a pair of hiking boots.

She's surprised and delighted as he hands her the boots.

MARTIN
In case you go hunting for any more crime scenes...Hope they fit.

ROBIN
Why thank you, Chief.

MARTIN
Now, I told you about that "chief" stuff. Just Jim, okay?

ROBIN
Okay Jim.

He smiles at her and she smiles back.

MARTIN
Okay...well...You wear them in good health, all right?

ROBIN
I will...Thanks.

He moves towards his vehicle.

MARTIN
Good night, Robin.

ROBIN
Good night, Jim.

MARTIN
This sounds like the *McNeil/Lehrer News Hour.*

She laughs and he climbs in and starts the car. He pulls out of the motel parking lot and waves. She opens her door and goes into her room.

II-16 INT/STAUF'S LIBRARY - NIGHT - BEFORE MIDNIGHT

[Trigger: Either entering the library anytime after Module Two is active or clicking on a certain title, say 'Justine' by the Marquis de Sade.] BRIAN DUTTON appears. He's holding the book, reading it casually, standing there in his suit, nodding...Then he stops, slowly turns, and faces the player.

DUTTON
Ah, didn't see you come in. Gave me a little fright, you did.

DUTTON looks back at the book.

DUTTON
Amazing thing, this. Absolutely amazing the things the Marquis has come up with, don't you think?

The library begins to dissolve into a darker chamber until it is transformed into a dungeon.

DUTTON (VO)
Absolutely amazing...

A woman is holding a large dog at bay with a heavy chain. She's wearing black tights and spike heels and she's naked from the waist up except for a studded collar.

It's Marie.

MARIE
SIT!

The dog sits.

MARIE (CONT'D)
Good boy...Now SPEAK!

As the dog opens its jaws the head morphs into the head of the motel desk clerk. His face contorts into an expression of horror and pain as he tries to speak but it comes out as a mournful howl. Marie laughs wickedly.

II-17 EXT/THE WOODS - DUSK [FLASHBACK]

The sound of Marie's laughter carries over.

A man is running through the woods. There are bloody scratches on his cheek. He glances over his shoulder, and then trips and falls to the ground. It's the same place Robin met Chief Martin—the murder scene.

MAN
No...please no. Please, oh, God—

He curls his legs underneath him, begging, as a glint of the afternoon sun gleams off the stainlees steel blade of a straight razor.

...END OF MODULE II

MODULE III SCENES—SAMANTHA'S STORY

III-1 INT / SAMANTHA FORD'S STUDIO - [4:15 p.m.]

Samantha, in her wheelchair, is creating a piece of video art on one of her monitors. She works the keyboard with remarkable intensity. A flurry of typing then a pause, staring at the work followed by another burst of activity. She wheels back for a different perspective, her eyes never leaving the monitor. Then she rushes forward and attacks the keyboard again. The image on the screen evolves, changes, intensifies. The sound of a door buzzer interrupts the process. Samantha pushes back from her work and wheels over to another monitor. She taps the keyboard and an image of Robin appears, as if she is on a surveillance camera, waiting outside of a door.

SAMANTHA
Yes?

ROBIN
Samantha Ford?

SAMANTHA
If you're selling anything I'm not interested. Please go away.

ROBIN
No, I just want to talk to you.

SAMANTHA
About what?

ROBIN
Eileen Wiley.

Samantha doesn't respond. She stares at the monitor, frozen.

ROBIN (CONT'D)
Hello...Are you still there?

Samantha just sits there.

On the monitor, Robin reaches for the doorbell and the buzzer sounds again.

SAMANTHA
Who are you?

ROBIN
My name is Robin Morales. I'm a producer for *Case Unsolved* and I'm researching a story on the Stauf Mansion...I was told you were there the night Eileen Wiley lost her hand.

SAMANTHA
Who told you that?

ROBIN
Doctor Thorton.

Samantha whispers to herself.

SAMANTHA
Oh God...

ROBIN
May I come in?

Samantha doesn't respond.

ROBIN (CONT'D)
Please.

Samantha types on the keyboard and the door opens.

Robin steps in and closes the door behind her. It's a large room and Samantha is at the far end.

SAMANTHA
What do you want from me, Ms. Morales?

ROBIN
The truth.

SAMANTHA
Whatever that is.

ROBIN
I want to know what really happened the night you and Eileen Wiley went to the Stauf Mansion.

Samantha sets her chair in motion and she heads across the room, straight at Robin.
She looks determined, threatening. Faster.

Robin stands her ground.

The chair skids to a stop just before colliding with Robin's legs. Samantha smiles.

SAMANTHA
Everyone knows what happened. Eileen got her hand bitten off by a guard dog.

ROBIN
Did you see it happen?

Samantha doesn't respond.

ROBIN
Did you?

There is some more silence before Samantha finally answers.

SAMANTHA
No.

ROBIN
I don't believe you.

SAMANTHA
So what?

ROBIN
What are you hiding?

SAMANTHA
Who do you think you are? Coming here from some moronic TV show speaking of the
truth. You don't care about the truth. You care about ratings. Now ain't THAT the truth!

Robin begins to walk around the room looking at the various video displays.

Samantha follows her.

ROBIN
This looks like very interesting work.

Samantha ignores the comment.

ROBIN (CONT'D)
Look, I'm sorry we got off to a bad start.

SAMANTHA
A bad start and a bad end. Please leave.

ROBIN
Do you think the current rash of murders and disappearances are connected to the House?

*Samantha, who has been following Robin past the video monitors, stops in her tracks. Robin
turns and looks at her. They just stare into each other's eyes without speaking.*

ROBIN
You do, don't you.

SAMANTHA
Get out.

ROBIN
I knew it! I'm on the right track.

SAMANTHA
Leave. Now.

Robin drops to her knees in front of Samantha and grasps the front of her chair.

ROBIN
Tell me what happened.

SAMANTHA
No.

ROBIN
What really happened to Eileen?

SAMANTHA
It was a dog. A vicious dog.

ROBIN
What about the two boys you followed there. They disappeared.

SAMANTHA
They never went there. They were runaways.

ROBIN
What happened to you? You haven't walked since that night.

SAMANTHA
I got sick.

ROBIN
But the doctors found nothing wrong with you. They say you just don't want to walk!

SAMANTHA
Get out! Get out!

Robin turns and walks slowly towards the door. She stops and looks back at Samantha, huddled in her chair.

ROBIN
It's been twenty years, Samantha. It's time you told the truth.

Samantha doesn't respond. Robin turns and leaves.

III-2 INT/STAUF HOUSE - NIGHT

Denning enters a room and finds a ghostly image of a young Samantha. She's curled into a fetal ball on the floor, whimpering. She looks up as Denning approaches her.

SAMANTHA
Please...Please don't hurt me.

He crouches next to her and reaches out to comfort her but she shrinks back.

SAMANTHA
No! No more.

DENNING
I'm not going to hurt you.

SAMANTHA
Where's Eileen?

DENNING
I don't know.

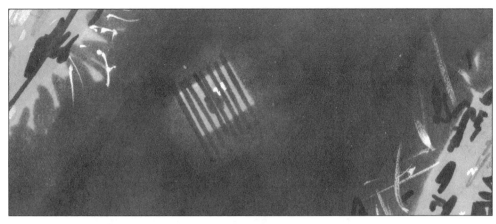

SAMANTHA
She ran away and left me...I couldn't move...

There's the sound of a far off scream.

SAMANTHA
That's her!

She scrambles to her feet.

SAMANTHA
This is all my fault!

She hurries from the room, her image fading as she goes.

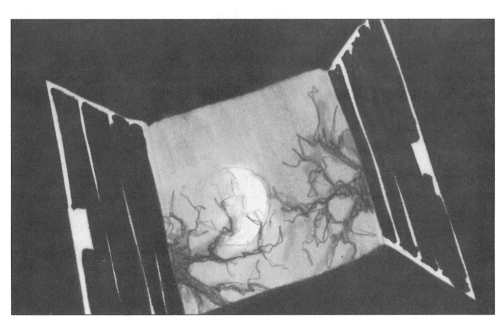

III-3 EXT/GATE - DAY

Chuck Lynch brings his aging Lincoln to a stop next to the gate to the mansion. He gets out and opens the trunk and, with a great deal of effort, he hoists a deer bag onto his shoulder. He leans against the gate, pushing it open with his shoulder and goes in.

III-4 EXT/MANSION - DAY

Chuck struggles up towards the mansion with his heavy burden.

III-5 EXT/MANSION PORCH - DAY

Lynch deposits the heavy sack on the dilapidated porch floor. He knocks three times and the door opens. He shoves the sack inside, pulls the door closed and hurries away into the night.

III-6 EXT/HARLEY INN - NIGHT

Samantha Ford wheels into the courtyard of the motel. Robin's convertible is parked next to a room and Samantha wheels up and knocks on the door. In a moment, Robin's voice comes from inside.

ROBIN
Who is it?

SAMANTHA
Samantha Ford.

The door opens.

SAMANTHA (CONT'D)
I've come to tell the truth...If you're ready for it.

ROBIN
What do you mean?

SAMANTHA
The truth may be more than you can stand.

Robin pushes the door open further.

ROBIN
Come in.

Samantha wheels through the doorway and Robin closes the door.

III-7 INT/ROBIN'S MOTEL ROOM - NIGHT

Robin sits on the edge of the bed next to Samantha in her wheel chair. Samantha looks distraught. She is about to speak then hesitates.

ROBIN
Can I get you something?

SAMANTHA
No, I...I just need to collect my thoughts.

ROBIN
I have some wine. Would you like some?

Samantha manages a smile.

SAMANTHA
I think I would.

Robin gets an open bottle from the dresser and fills two plastic motel cups. She returns to the bed and hands a cup to Samantha.

ROBIN
Cheers.

SAMANTHA
Thank you...What happened on that terrible night twenty years ago...There isn't a day that goes by that my thoughts haven't been haunted by the memory...Everything that's happened since, every breath I take is influenced by that night.

ROBIN
Do you mind if I record this.

SAMANTHA
I don't mind.

Robin reaches into her bag and takes out a cassette recorder, clicks it on and places it on the bed.

ROBIN
Please...continue.

SAMANTHA

Eileen and I went to the house to find Peter and Charlie—the two boys who supposedly disappeared. They were going to break in to the Stauf Mansion—the so-called "haunted house" and...well, I was pretty wild as a teenager. Eileen didn't want to go but I talked her into it...She always did everything I did and...Oh god...what happened to her...It's all my fault.

ROBIN

Do you want to stop?

SAMANTHA

No. If I do, I don't know if I could start again...We...We were...raped.

ROBIN

Oh no! Those boys?

SAMANTHA

No...the...I'm sorry...

Robin reaches for her hand.

ROBIN

It's okay.

Samantha takes a moment to re-compose herself. She takes a deep breath then looks at Robin and speaks in a calm voice.

SAMANTHA

We were raped by the house.

Robin is speechless. They just look at each other. Samantha breaks the silence.

SAMANTHA (CONT'D)

So now you think I'm totally out of my mind.

ROBIN

No, I...

SAMANTHA

Yes you do...Here's this crazy lady in a wheelchair raving about how she was raped by a house.

ROBIN

I...I don't know what to think.

SAMANTHA

Think what you want...But I'll tell you...that house is not what it appears to be...it's a living thing!..It's a house or it's Henry Stauf or some ungodly creature...It's impossible to describe...and impossible to believe but I KNOW what happened to me!

ROBIN

But how?

SAMANTHA

I don't know how...We were in the house and suddenly I couldn't move—as if something invisible were holding me. I couldn't see it but I was in its grip...I could feel it all over me...touching me. I started screaming and Eileen got scared and ran.

III-8 EXT/GATE - NIGHT

A young Eileen is running down the overgrown path to the gate, away from the sounds of screaming.

The gate begins to close on its own. Eileen reaches the gate when it's almost closed. She tries to pull it open and the gate traps her hand. She screams as the iron bars squeeze tighter, tearing the skin, ripping the flesh and bone.

III -9 INT/ROBIN'S ROOM - NIGHT

ROBIN

How did you get away?

SAMANTHA

When it was finished with us, it simply let us go and I got Eileen to Doctor Thorton...But the worst was yet to come...Whatever it was—the thing—I...I became pregnant...We both did.

ROBIN

Oh my god...

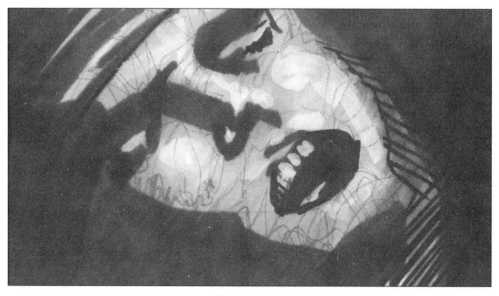

SAMANTHA

I decided to have an abortion. Eileen was scared to go through with it but I...
It was a back-alley thing and...

She begins to get upset again.

ROBIN

It's okay. You've said enough. Don't...

SAMANTHA

No, I have to finish this...I got a very serious infection and...the result was what you see. I
suffered irreparable nerve damage and I'm confined to a wheelchair.

ROBIN

I can't imagine such horror.

Samantha becomes suddenly intense.

SAMANTHA

Eileen lives the true horror—she gave birth to Marie! I'd rather spend my life in a
wheelchair than have a child like that. She's always been evil—the bad seed—but Hell itself
has been unleashed since her eighteenth birthday. She's behind the violent happenings in
this valley...Whatever evil that house might be—Marie is its offspring...She's the one...She's
the daughter of the Devil himself.

Samantha turns her chair and begins to wheel towards the door.

SAMANTHA (CONT'D)

It's crazy...A house! Pure insanity...But it's true...Just ask Eileen.

She opens the door and leaves.

III-10 THE STAUF HOUSE - NIGHT

Denning walks down the hallway and stops—

DENNING

Man, does it stink in this place.

The VOICE again, whispering...

VOICE

Like that dead raccoon your father found in the basement.

DENNING

Say what?

He pulls his game book out of his pocket and flips it open.

DENNING

You trying to tell me something?

He tries to switch the computer on but gets no response. Suddenly there's laughter, girlish giggles. He turns around, looking for the source of the sound. More laughter, and a bedroom door opens... Denning goes through the door and the door remains open while control returns to the player.

III-11 MARTINE BURDEN'S BEDROOM - NIGHT

Denning enters a dark room covered with decades of dust. A rat scurries in the corner, disappearing into a hole. He hears the laughter again.

DENNING

Robin?

Martine Burden appears in a low-cut, strapless gown. The room suddenly becomes filled with light and is magically restored to its original elegance.

DENNING

Wow!

BURDEN

Oh, you like it?

She wriggles her shoulders with a seductive smile.

DENNING

Uh...Yeah!

BURDEN

I hoped you would. I wore it just for you.

DENNING

Well...thanks.

BURDEN

So do you think there's a role for me in your new play?...Am I right for the part?

DENNING

I...uh...I don't know...

BURDEN

I'd be very grateful.

She puts her arms around his neck and smiles seductively.

BURDEN (CONT'D)

Very grateful...

She kisses him and presses against him.

He pushes her back.

BURDEN

What's the matter?...You don't like me?...You don't want me in your play?

DENNING

No...It's not that I don't...

BURDEN

I know I'm right for the role...I can give you more.

She begins to remove her dress.

DENNING

No...Please...Where's Robin?

BURDEN

Who's Robin?...Why do you want her?...WHAT'S WRONG WITH ME!

She reaches up and touches her face. The skin begins to peel and flake. She TRANSFORMS into a skeleton, still talking.

> BURDEN
>
> *Please, take me out of here.*
>
> *The skeleton reaches out to Denning.*
>
> BURDEN(CONT'D)
>
> Please, take me with you...before—before—
>
> *Her voice deepens, darken, turning into a guttural HOWL—*
>
> BURDEN(CONT'D)
>
> It's too late.
>
> *The skeleton disappears. The room fades into its original state.*

III-12 INT/COFFEE SHOP - NIGHT

> *Robin takes a seat at the counter.*
>
> *The place is empty except for a small group in the corner booth.*
>
> *Eileen is behind the counter. She looks up and smiles at Robin then the smile quickly disappears when she realizes who she is.*
>
> EILEEN
>
> You looking for food or information?
>
> ROBIN
>
> I've spoken with Samantha Ford.
>
> EILEEN
>
> So?
>
> ROBIN
>
> She told me an unbelievable story.
>
> EILEEN
>
> So don't believe it.
>
> *There is an awkward silence as they stare at each other.*
>
> ROBIN
>
> May I have some coffee?
>
> EILEEN
>
> Sure.
>
> *She pours a cup and hands it to Robin. Eileen lights a cigarette and offers the pack to Robin who shakes her head.*
>
> EILEEN(CONT'D)
>
> So what's the story about?

ROBIN
It's about two girls and a house that isn't a house at all...and there's no dog.

Eileen takes a moment to respond.

EILEEN
What else?

ROBIN
The two girls got pregnant. One of them had an abortion—which left her paralyzed—and one gave birth to a girl named Marie which according to Samantha is a worse fate than spending your life in a wheelchair.

Eileen's eyes begin to well with tears.

ROBIN (CONT'D)
The house in this story is something that lives ...Something evil and Marie is, somehow, the daughter of this evil.

EILEEN
Don't say that!

ROBIN
And she's behind the horrific murders and...

EILEEN
Stop it! That's a lie.

ROBIN
What about the rest of this fantastic story, Eileen?

EILEEN
That's just what it is—a story...How could anyone believe such a thing?

ROBIN
Samantha was so sure.

EILEEN
Samantha always had a good imagination.

ROBIN
Is there any truth in what she says?

There is a long pause before Eileen answers.

EILEEN
No.

ROBIN
Then what really happened to your hand?

Another pause, then finally Eileen gives her a very direct look.

EILEEN
It got bitten off by a dog.

*Robin returns the directness of the look and they both stare at each other, both knowing that
Eileen is lying.*

ROBIN
I don't believe you.

EILEEN
And I don't care.

ROBIN
What is it about the house Eileen? What's it really all about?

EILEEN
Why don't you just go there yourself?

Another silence as they continue to confront each other's stares.

EILEEN (CONT'D)
You're afraid, aren't you?

*Robin doesn't respond. She whirls off the stool and leaves without another word. A woman
in the corner booth turns around and gives Eileen a chilling look. It's Marie.*

END OF MODULE III

MODULE IV SCENES

IV-1 INT/MOTEL ROOM - NIGHT

Marie is anxiously pacing back and forth in the motel room. All of her cool demeanor and slow sensuality has disappeared. The door opens and Chuck comes in, excited.

CHUCK
Hey, Sweet Marie.

Marie whirls around with a knife in her hand and looks at him with menace in her eyes.

MARIE
It's that time again.

Chuck's excitement rapidly disappears.

CHUCK
So soon? But Marie, I just...

MARIE
Shut up!...Just take this knife and get that TV producer.

Chuck looks terrified.

CHUCK
Oh...I...I can't do that, Marie...Not her...I...

Marie is verging on hysteria.

MARIE
What do you mean you CAN'T! You'll DO it! And you know what'll happen to you
if you don't!

CHUCK
Please...Marie...She's too well known...People will come looking for her.

MARIE
I don't care!

CHUCK
Marie, just listen to what you're saying...

MARIE
No YOU listen! Do you really want to say no to Stauf?

Chuck freezes then slowly shakes his head.

CHUCK
No, I don't.

MARIE

Then take this knife and do what you've been told to do.

Reluctantly, Chuck crosses the room and takes the knife from her.

MARIE

Good boy, Chuck. You had me worried.

CHUCK

Don't have to worry about ol' Chucky, baby.

He reaches for her but she pushes him off.

MARIE (CONT'D)

Get away from me.

CHUCK

But I thought...

MARIE

Later...Do this first...Now go!

Disappointed, he turns and leaves.

IV-2 EXT/ROBIN'S MOTEL ROOM - EARLY MORNING

Chuck slinks up to the room with the convertible parked in front. He looks around to see if he's being watched, then quickly inserts a key in the lock and steps inside.

IV-3 INT/ROBIN'S MOTEL ROOM - EARLY MORNING

The shades are drawn and the room is semi-lit with the first grey light of early morning. Chuck peers into the semi-darkness at the mounded covers on the bed. He hesitates, frightened and unsure.

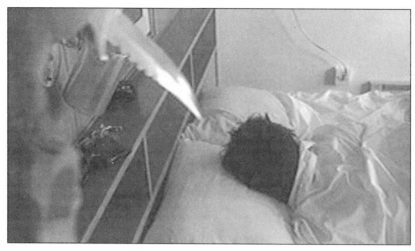

Suddenly he rushes at the bed with the knife held high and brings it down with a deadly force. The blade penetrates the bedclothes and buries itself in flesh. Chuck tears back the covers and is overcome with a look of shock. A red stain is spreading over the naked chest of Chief Martin, the knife buried in his heart. Chuck looks panicked. He hears a noise coming from the bathroom.

IV-4 INT/BATHROOM - DAY

Robin is showering behind a frosted glass partition.

IV-5 INT/ROBIN'S ROOM -DAY

Chuck is listening at the bathroom door. He goes back to the bed and pulls at the knife in Martin's chest. He struggles with it, unable to pull it out.

IV-6 INT/BATHROOM- DAY

Robin steps out of the shower, wrapping herself in a towel.

IV-7 INT/ROBIN'S ROOM - DAY

Chuck takes Martin's clothes from the back of a chair and tosses them on the bed then wraps up Martin and his clothes in a blood-stained sheet and hoists the bundle onto his shoulder. Staggering under the weight, Chuck makes his way to the door and leaves. The bathroom door opens and Robin comes out wrapped in the towel, having heard the front door close.

ROBIN
Jim?

She sees that he's gone. She looks perplexed and a little disappointed. She shrugs and goes back into the bathroom.

IV-8 EXT/MANSION - DAY

Chuck struggles with his heavy burden in the overgrown field approaching the mansion.

IV-9 EXT/MANSION PORCH - DAY

Chuck drops his bloody bundle on the porch and knocks on the door. This time when he pushes the bundle in, Chuck gets pulled in with it.

IV-10 INT/INSIDE THE STAUF MANSION - NIGHT

Chuck finds himself in the kitchen.

JULIA HEINE is at the table cutting something with a cleaver. She is dressed as she was in THE 7TH GUEST, except the dress is faded, tattered and stained. She whacks at whatever she's cutting...She looks up at Chuck.

JULIA
Are you ready?

CHUCK
For what?

JULIA
Soup's on.

Stauf suddenly appears.

STAUF
Soup's on!

A head emerges from the soup pot.

HEAD
Soup's on!

The kitchen starts to change, the walls turning a deep red, shiny, dripping. And in the cascade of red blood streaming off the walls, onto the floor, there are faces, screaming faces in the wall, looking out, begging. Chuck begins to scream. Julia comes towards Chuck, her meat cleaver dripping blood.

JULIA
How 'bout a Chuck roast?

Stauf laughs.

STAUF
Chuck steak!

HEAD
Chuck him into the soup!

The cleaver comes down.

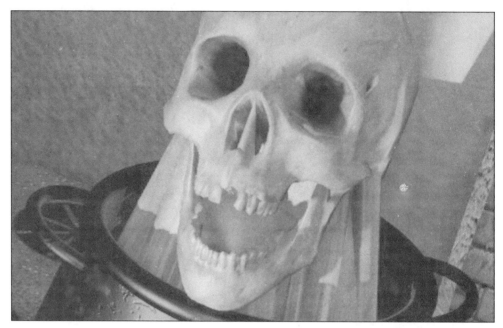

IV-11EXT/GATE - DAY

Robin pulls up in her convertible outside the rusted gate to the Stauf Mansion.

IV-12 EXT/MANSION - DAY

Robin makes her way through the weeds, approaching the house. She's dressed in jeans and a T-shirt and her new hiking boots.

IV-13 EXT/MANSION PORCH - DAY

Robin climbs the steps onto the porch. She sniffs the air, recoiling at some foul odor.

Tentatively, she reaches for the door handle and as her hand is about to come in contact with the rusted metal, the door unlatches itself and creaks open. She peers into the darkness inside.

IV-14 INT/SAMANTHA'S STUDIO - DAY

Samantha is watching Robin at the mansion on one of her monitors.

SAMANTHA
Don't do it...

IV-15 EXT/MANSION - DAY

Robin hesitates, then swallows her fear and steps over the rotting threshold. The door slams closed behind her.

IV-16 INT/ SAMANTHA FORD'S STUDIO - DAY

The sound of the slamming door is carried over and echos in the studio. Samantha watches the monitor with tears in her eyes.

SAMANTHA
Oh, God...

She slumps back in her wheelchair, defeated.

END OF MODULE IV

MODULE V SCENES

V-1 THE STAUF HOUSE - NIGHT

ROBIN moves slowly through the dark, upstairs hallway, past the PAINTINGS, which react to her steps...glistening, pulsating, watching...She comes to the end of the hallway—and stops. There are doors surrounding her. She hears a noise behind her and whirls around to see a small cat. The cat meows and Robin backs up a bit. She hears a whispered voice...the voice of Henry Stauf.

STAUF (VO)
You don't like cats, do you Robin?

ROBIN
Who's there?

STAUF (VO)
You've been afraid of them since you were a little girl.

The cat moves towards her.

STAUF (VO)
Ever since you and your sister drowned the kitten in the toilet.

ROBIN
How did you know...

The cat hisses, cutting her off.

STAUF
Poor little kitty.

ROBIN
I didn't mean to kill it.

STAUF
Poor little dead kitty.

The cat morphs into a full grown mountain lion.

STAUF
Here kitty kitty.

ROBIN
No!

The cougar snarls and moves toward Robin. She screams as the big cat comes closer. Robin is about to crumble. Just as the cougar reaches her, it vanishes.

V-2 THE STAUF HOUSE - NIGHT

[Note: The scene is triggered upon entering the library anytime after Module Five has been opened.] EDWARD KNOX appears, holding a brandy. The room is slowly filled with a warm glow, and becomes renewed...as it was decades ago, Knox appears suddenly startled, and turns to face the player.

KNOX
Oh—sorry...didn't see you come in.
He looks at his glass of brandy.

KNOX (CONT'D)
Just sampling something from Stauf's cellar. Would you—

(a beat)

I guess not. After all, you don't have time for that, now do you?

He comes closer...

KNOX
You're looking for her. I know(conspiratorial wink). We all know that—But you see—someone's coming for YOU. You can't get out—have you tried the front door...It's quite impossible...And now—You'd better—

With the next word, Knox's head EXPLODES.

KNOX (CONT'D)
Hide!

And the library returns to its normal state.

V-3 INT/ THE STAUF HOUSE-THE NURSERY - NIGHT

Robin walks into the nursery, the toys covered with dust. She examines the puppets, the dolls, the toy trucks. Robin picks up one of the dolls...It starts to move,

smiling, talking...

DOLL
I—I want my mommy—

She drops the doll.

A voice comes from behind her.

VOICE(V/O)
'I want my mommy...'

Robin spins around and sees Henry Stauf standing in the room.

STAUF
And what do you want?

He takes a step into the room.

STAUF(CONT'D)
Not your mommy...I'd guess.

Robin backs up.

ROBIN
Who are you?

STAUF
Success...power...influence. Money...fame...

Another step.

STAUF (CONT'D)
Some of us want even more than that...

The nursery begins to glow, restored, as Stauf comes
closer to Robin.

STAUF (CONT'D)
I thought that all I wanted was money, enough wealth for a lifetime or two...But that was
only the beginning. And all that IT wanted...all the HOUSE wanted in return was merely
to—exist. But like so may things, to exist it needs to be fed—

Robin looks horrified.

ROBIN
What are you talking about?

STAUF (CONT'D)
To live it must eat. That's not so much to want, now is it?

Stauf is right next to Robin.

STAUF (CONT'D)
And what is it that you want...What can the house...My house...give you?
Money...success...power...

ROBIN
How can a house give anything to anyone?

STAUF
Never doubt the power of this house. You've seen its magic.

ROBIN
You're saying I can have anything I want?

STAUF
Name it.

ROBIN
I—

V-4 INT/SAMANTHA'S STUDIO - NIGHT

Samantha is watching Robin and Stauf on her monitor.

SAMANTHA
No! Don't say it!

She types furiously on her keyboard.

V-5 INT/STAUF HOUSE HALLWAY - NIGHT

Denning's gamebook starts beeping.

DENNING
It's about time.

He pulls the gamebook out of his jacket and flips it open.
The small screen shows Robin and Stauf.

STAUF
Just tell me what you want. The world is yours.

DENNING
Robin!

ROBIN
Carl?

V-6 INT/NURSERY - NIGHT

Robin is looking around for Carl's voice.

ROBIN
Carl? Where are you?

STAUF
Never mind him. He's just an illusion. Tell me what you want. Your own show...
Your own network?

Her eyes grow wide.

ROBIN
My own network?

Stauf snaps his fingers.

STAUF
Like that! Is that what you want?

Denning's voice echoes in the room.

DENNING (VO)
Robin!

STAUF
Is it?

ROBIN
I...

STAUF
Say it!

DENNING (VO)
Don't!

V-7 INT/HALLWAY - NIGHT

Denning watches Robin on the screen of his gamebook. The image fades.

DENNING
Robin!

Samantha's face appears on the screen.

SAMANTHA
She's gone.

DENNING
Who are you?

SAMANTHA
Samantha. I'm the one who sent you the gamebook. I've been trying
to help you save Robin.

DENNING
Why are you doing this?

SAMANTHA
I thought...hoped...you could defeat the house but the house is too powerful...and we are all
so weak...You've got to get out now.

DENNING
I can't leave her here.

Robin's voice comes from another room. She's screaming for help.

ROBIN (OS)
Help! Carl, help me!

SAMANTHA
Don't go! It's too late!

DENNING
I've got to!

ROBIN (OS)
Carl!

SAMANTHA
Don't do it! The temptation will be too much for you.

DENNING
See ya later, Samantha.

*He snaps the book closed and stuffs it back into his pocket as he runs down the hall
towards Robin's voice.*

V-8 INT. TEMPLE'S BEDROOM -NIGHT [REALTIME]

Denning rushes in, hearing the screams of Robin.

ROBIN (OS)
Oh, God—help. Please, no more—no!

DENNING
Robin!

But he enters the room, and there's no one there. Nothing. The door slams behind him. There is a rumble, the sound of the house fully alive, a deep bass note that swells.

Denning slowly turns. And as he turns we see three doors...and each door begins to open...slowly...

END OF MODULE V

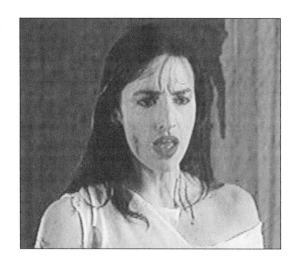

Warning! Spoiler!

What follows is the original script for the end of the game.
If you don't want to know what happens at the end,
DO NOT READ ANY FURTHER!

ENDGAME

[The opening sequence of the Endgame is triggered after all scenes of Module Five have been witnessed. Then the final choices are presented...]

E-1 INT. THE STAUF MANSION - NIGHT [11:00 P.M.]

DENNING stands facing the three doors. Stauf materializes in front of the doors.

STAUF
Hello Carl Denning and welcome to LET'S MAKE A REAL DEAL!

DENNING
Who the hell are you?

STAUF
Why, I'm Monty Stauf, your host on LET'S MAKE A REAL DEAL and have I got a real
deal for you...I wonder what this is in my pocket...

(He reaches into his pocket and pulls out a wad of money.)

...SIX, COUNT 'EM, SIX HUNDRED DOLLARS!
He peels off six bills and hands them to Denning.

STAUF (CONT'D)
Now, Carl, here's the deal: You can keep the six hundred dollars but you must choose a
door, be it door number 1, 2 or 3...OR you can pay me two hundred dollars and see what's
behind the door of your choice. What'll it be, Carl?

DENNING
I'll pay.

He gives Stauf two hundred.

STAUF
Thank you. Now which door?

DENNING
The one in the middle.

STAUF

Okay! Let's see what's behind door number two!

The door opens to reveal a large television set.

STAUF

A big screen TV! Isn't this fun Carl? Now, let's make another deal. You can keep the TV AND the four hundred dollars you have left or you can pay me two hundred dollars to see what's behind another door.

Denning gives Stauf another two hundred.

DENNING

Let's see what's behind number one.

STAUF

All right! What a player! Door number one!

The door opens to reveal Marie. She's sitting on a chair dressed in a black bra and panties, garter belt, stockings and high heels.

STAUF

It's sweet Marie! She can be absolutely yours anytime, night or day!

MARIE

Anytime.

STAUF

Imagine the hours of fun and enjoyment you'll have with Marie! A lot more exciting than watching TV.

MARIE

You can watch me if you like.

She places her hands on her knees and trails her fingers up the inside of her thighs. She licks her lips and smiles. Suddenly the big screen TV flickers to life and Samantha appears on the screen.

SAMANTHA

Be strong, Carl Denning. Don't give in to temptation.

STAUF

Damn it! I thought that TV was unplugged!

SAMANTHA

Choose me.

STAUF

What a choice! Marie—sweet, sensuous, sexy Marie—or Samantha in a wheelchair! Hah!

DENNING

What's behind door number three?

Stauf extends his arm and rubs his fingers together.

STAUF
Pay up.

Denning gives him the last two hundred dollars.

STAUF (CONT'D)
Door number three!

The third door opens and Robin is there.

ROBIN
Carl, I've been so frightened. Please, choose me. Save me. I love you.

MARIE
I'll give you anything you want...Anything and everything.

SAMANTHA
Don't listen to them. You'll be lost forever.

STAUF
Shut up, Samantha!

SAMANTHA
He's afraid of you, Carl. Choose me. Destroy the power of this hellish house.

ROBIN
Carl, you have to choose me. After all we've been through...I need you Carl.

MARIE
Anytime...anyplace..any way you want me.

Stauf confronts the player.

STAUF
Well, what'll it be, sport? The choice is yours...

CUT TO:
THE DOORS.

> # Last Warning!
>
> You really don't want to read any further unless you want to see the actual ending sequences. This is your last chance to stop reading and go play the game. We warned you!

E-2 INT. TEMPLE'S ROOM - NIGHT

(Triggered by choosing Robin)

Note: All choices should be made real choices—all saved positions from Mod Five on will be erased after choosing. The Player is told this. They can eventually see all three endings—but not before re-experiencing the last part of the game...

Denning chooses Robin's door. He enters and they embrace. There are tears in her eyes.

ROBIN
Thank God.

DENNING
Let's go home.

E-3 INT/DENNING'S COUNTRY HOME - DAY

Robin is in Denning's living room watching a newscast on TV. A woman anchorperson is reading the news.

ANCHOR
The body of TV reporter Carl Denning was found floating in the Hudson river today. Denning disappeared during his honeymoon in Harley-On-Hudson after his celebrated marriage to Robin Morales, newly appointed president of the Stauf Broadcasting System.

Robin watches without emotion. She clicks a button on a remote control and the picture fades to black.

E-4 INT. TEMPLE'S ROOM - NIGHT (TRIGGERED BY CHOOSING MARIE)

Denning moves towards Marie's door. She gets up from her chair and walks away into the darkness beyond, looking over her shoulder with a seductive smile. Denning enters the door and follows her.

E-5 INT/BEDROOM - NIGHT

Denning enters a bedroom. Marie is on the bed, lounging back, inviting. Denning gets on the foot of the bed and crawls up on top of her. He kisses her and she responds passionately which unleashes a hunger in him. She rolls him over so that she is straddling him. She kisses his neck and chest and unbuttons his shirt as she works her way down. Denning looks down at the mane of hair cascading over his stomach. She looks up at him –but it isn't Marie. It's Stauf in a wig!

STAUF
What a deal!

Denning screams. THE REST OF THE SCENE IS PLAYED INTO THE CAMERA AS PLAYER'S POV. Stauf rolls off the bed and grabs a barbecued rib from a plate on a dresser. He tosses the wig onto the bed.

STAUF
I'll let you in on a secret—'cause you're so special (smacks his lips) Mmmm... these are good...

He laughs. He offers up a rib.

STAUF (CONT'D)
Like a bite?...Some choice you made, huh?   Oh, don't look so sad. I'm not so bad...See?

Stauf morphs back into Marie, still eating the rib, red sauce dripping off her chin onto her chest. More lip-smacking. She holds out the rib, nearly finished.

MARIE/STAUF
Sure, you wouldn't like a bite...? After all(she laughs)...It's you!

Marie laughs uproariously and the laughing voice begins to sound like Stauf's then she morphs back into Stauf, laughing, doubling over. He begins to cough and it becomes a disgusting, choking sound. As he chokes, he begins to change into his native form—the alien creature that's been behind this all along. It looks up, jaws open, salivating—as it leaps, devouring the player into blackness.

E-5-PG INT/BEDROOM - NIGHT [PG VERSION]

Marie leads Denning into a bedroom holding his hand. When they reach the bed, she pulls him close and they tumble to the mattress. He kisses her and she responds passionately. She rolls him over so that she is on top. She kisses his neck and chest and unbuttons his shirt as she works her way down. Denning looks down at the mane of hair cascading over his stomach. She looks up at him—but it isn't Marie.

...etc.

E-6 INT. TEMPLE'S ROOM - NIGHT (TRIGGERED BY CHOOSING SAM)

Denning moves towards the middle door containing the TV with Samantha's image. He reaches to touch the screen and there is an explosion of white light.

E-7 INT/SAMANTHA FORD'S STUDIO - DAY

Denning finds himself in Samantha's studio. Samantha looks up at him, sitting in her wheelchair next to one of her monitors. She looks more relaxed than anytime before. She smiles.

SAMANTHA
Welcome, Carl Denning. You made the right choice.

DENNING
It wasn't easy.

SAMANTHA
No.

DENNING
I hated leaving Robin behind.

SAMANTHA
I know. You risked your life for her...But it was too late to save her.

DENNING
So what happens now?

She extends her hand.

SAMANTHA
Come and see.

He takes her hand and stands behind her as they both look at the monitor. On the screen, the Stauf Mansion is engulfed in flames.

SAMANTHA
You won, Carl.

DENNING
What about Robin?

Samantha shakes her head.

SAMANTHA
She was lost the moment she said yes to Stauf.

They watch the monitor as the house burns.

There are tears in Denning's eyes. Samantha looks content, virtually radiating an inner peace. It's been a long battle for her. On the monitor, there is nothing left but blackness.

THE END

THE 11TH HOUR
THE QUICK
WALKTHROUGH

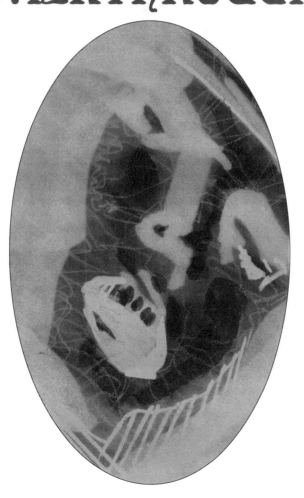

CHAPTER EIGHT

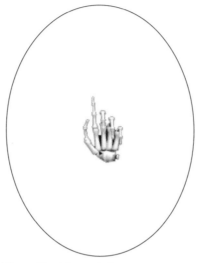

Quick Walkthrough

On the following pages you'll find a linear walkthrough of *The 11th Hour: The Sequel to The 7th Guest*. During treasure hunting, it is important to note that rooms are inert until the room's puzzles are defeated. Once a room is activated, all of its contents will become selectable for treasure hunting and will remain so throughout the rest of the evening up to the 11th Hour.

Finding the correct treasure hunt object will often elicit a reward in the shape of an animation and/or video scene. The resulting video will be shown at resolution of 640x320 pixels. These clips are replayable from the GameBook.

At the end of each hour, when the AI game has been defeated, the GameBook will display a thumbnail screen of the current Hour's section of video. Upon pressing the play button, the video run until the end of the Hour's section.

Everything you need to know to get through the game is listed below. Do the steps in order, treasure hunts and puzzles, and you'll make it to the end of the game by the most efficient and ideal path. Use this quick walkthrough only if you get lost, or if you really don't want to challenge yourself. Otherwise, you'll cheat yourself of all the fun of exploration. Remember, nothing really bad will happen if you wander around. You might solve some of the puzzles out of sequence, but that's all right.

* = Puzzle

Item	**Location**	**Triggers**
7 P.M.		
Tonic Water	Library	Robin in Coffee Shop
*Cash Register Puzzle	Dutton's Room	Opens Dutton's; Picture Gallery
Cork	Dutton's Room	Cork anim.; Robin & Eileen
*Horseplay Puzzle	Foyer	Open Foyer/Hallway
Satyr	Picture Gallery	Marie in Motel Office
*Book Puzzle	Library	Opens Library
Globe	Library	Globe anim.; Robin/blood on rocks
*Amazing Labyrinth	Laboratory	AI game; opens Laboratory
Tablet	Laboratory	Bloody face on ground
Redbreast (Robin)	Foyer	Robin in painting
*Mondrian Painting AI	Picture Gallery	End of module AI puzzle
8 P.M.		
Desk	Library	Desk animation
Torso	Picture Gallery	Robin meets Marie
Liquor	Dutton's Room	Cork animation
*Number Chain Puzzle	Game Room	Unlocks Game Room
Irish Setter	Game Room	Robin interviews Doc Thorton
Grandfather Clock	Foyer	Pendulum; Denning & ghost Eileen
*Four Spiders Puzzle	Bathroom	Unlock Bathroom & Dining Room
Straight Razor	Bathroom	Razor; Chuck & Marie at dam
Orange	Dining Room	Morphing image (in painting)
*Sliding Mirror Puzzle	Knox's Room	Opens Knox's Room & Chapel
Nightmare	Knox's Room	Robin runs into Jim
Great Dane	Library	Library scene
*Centaur (Gryphon) AI	Chapel	End of module AI puzzle

9 P.M.

Television	Dutton's Room	Robin meets Samantha
Organ	Chapel	Organ plays
*Railroad Switcher	Attic	Unlock Attic
Ivory Tower (Rook)	Attic	Denning meets ghostly Samantha
Torch	Chapel	Sparks; Chuck drops off body
*Ten Plates Stacked	Kitchen	Unlock Kitchen
Grater	Kitchen	Crawling fingers
Disc	Laboratory	Disc anim.; Samantha visits Robin
Toothpaste	Bathroom	Toothpaste creature
*Cubed Dice Puzzle	Temple's Room	Unlock Temple's Room
Guillotine	Temple's Room	Guillotine anim.; Eileen & gate
Gardenia	2nd floor Hall	Denning walking up hallway
*Labyrinth Puzzle	Burden's Room	Unlock Burden's Room
Rose	Burden's Room	Petal falls; Denning meets Burden
*Necklace Puzzle	Heine's Room	Unlock Heine's & Room at Top
Earring	Heine's Room	Ear animation
*Beehive AI	Room at Top	End of module AI puzzle

10 P.M.

*Moving House Puzzle	Music Room	Unlock Music Room (piano gone)
Harp	Music Room	Harp strings
Nutcracker	Hallway	Nutcracker; Marie pacing room
Eyeball	Game Room	Eyeball rolls
Blade	Temple's Room	Chuck stalks sleeping figure
Locomotive	Attic	Train animation
Sheets	Burden's Room	Chuck pulled into house
Cleaver	Kitchen	Cleaver; Soup's On video
*Trilobite AI	Dining Room	End of module AI puzzle

11 P.M.

Lion	Hallway	Cougar attacks Robin
Port	Knox's Room	Knox speaks
*Switchboard Puzzle	Doll Room	Opens Doll Room/access Nursery
Rattle	Nursery	Rattle; Robin in Nursery
XI	Foyer (on clock)	Robin on Samantha's monitor
Inkstand	Library	Pen writes message (clue)
*Miniature Kitchen AI	Nursery	End of module AI puzzle

End of Game sequence

THE 11TH HOUR

THE PUZZLES

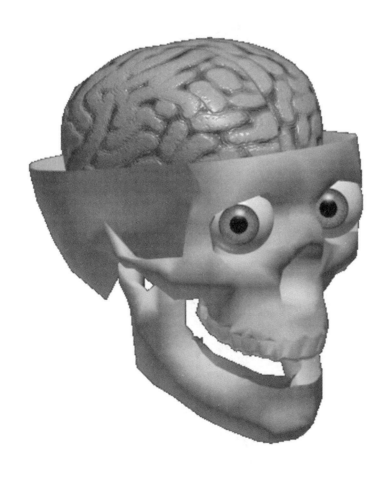

CHAPTER NINE

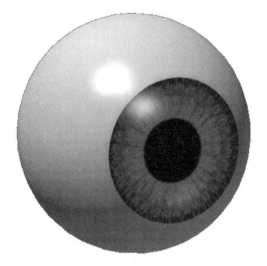

Puzzle Solutions

In this section you'll find the best puzzle solutions we could come up with. In the case of the logical puzzles, we're pretty sure we've got the best solutions there are. If you find a better one, let us know! As far as the artificial intelligence puzzles, the ones you play directly against Stauf, we've given you the best information we have, but there are no sure-fire solutions, unless specifically noted. In other words, you're on your own when it comes to solving the AI puzzles.

Please use these solutions only as a next-to-last resort—just before you have Samantha solve the puzzles for you. Too much reliance on these solutions can reduce the amount of fun you'll have playing the game, and we wouldn't want that to happen, now would we?

Generally, have fun, use solutions when you really need them, and otherwise, try to keep your wits about you. And, whatever you do, don't let Stauf win!

Puzzle #1

Book Checkers (Library)

Clues

  #1a Put all green books on the right shelf and all the red books
       on the left.

  #1b Put all red books on the right shelf and all the green books
       on the left.

  #1c Put all the red books on one side and all the green books
       on the other.

  #2   You can move adjacent pairs only.

  #3   It must be done in four moves.

Solution

Move 2 & 3 to 9 & 10

Move 5 & 6 to 2 & 3

Move 8 & 9 to 5 & 6

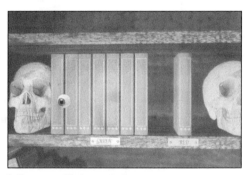

Move 1 & 2 to 8 & 9

Puzzle #2

Cash Register (Dutton's Room)

Clues

- #1   Divide the keys into two halves of the same shape.
- #2   Each half must contain the same amount of money.
- #3.   The amount needed in each half is eighty-one cents.

Solution

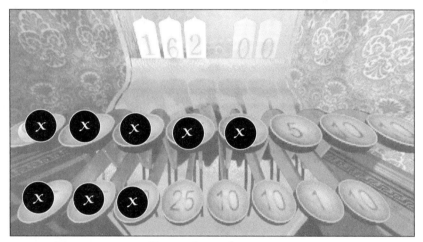

Press these keys. . .

. . . to get this final move. Or try the mirror image keys!

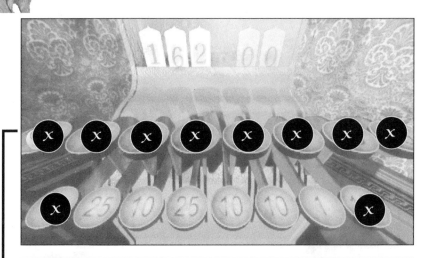

Alternate
Solutions

Puzzle #3

Horseplay (Foyer)

Clues

#1   Exchange the positions of the white and black knights
      using standard knight moves.

#2   You can't move a knight off this odd section of chessboard.

#3   I think I could do it in 40 moves.

Note: In the solution that follows, each pair of images represents the starting and ending moves of a particular knight, with the full description of moves listed below the pictures.

Solution

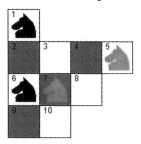

Moves 1-4:
1⇒4⇒10⇒2⇒8

Moves 5-8:
7⇒1⇒4⇒10⇒2

Moves 9-12:
5⇒7⇒1⇒4⇒10

Move 13-16:
6⇒4⇒1⇒7⇒5

Move 17-19:
10⇒4⇒1⇒7

Moves 20-22:
2⇒10⇒4⇒1

Moves 23-26:
8⇒2⇒10⇒4⇒6

Move 27-29:
1⇒4⇒10⇒2

Move 30-32:
7⇒1⇒4⇒10

Moves 33-35:
6⇒4⇒1⇒7

Move 36-37:
10⇒4⇒1

Moves 38-40:
2⇒10⇒4⇒6

Puzzle #4

Amazing Labyrinth (Laboratory)

Clues
- #1   You're playing against Stauf.
- #2   Build a path for the mouse to find the orange hole.
- #3   Placing a maze piece causes the other pieces in the row to slide over or a column to slide up and down.

Note: This puzzle has no easy or definite solution. One trick you can try, however is that of resetting the puzzle until you find an opening configuration that looks good (see page 245). There's some luck to this, but if you get a good opening, you can often solve this one in just a couple of moves. In general, however, you'll probably find this one of the most frustrating puzzles in the game.

Solution

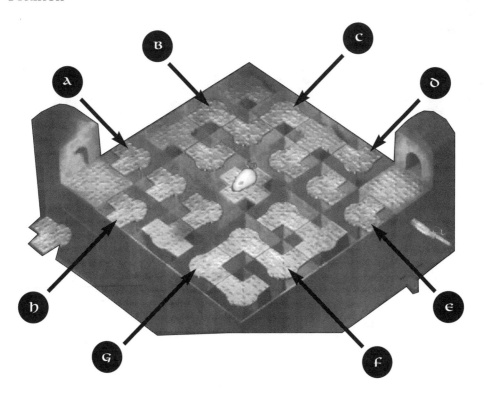

Another Mousetrap Solution

Here's how the puzzle looked at the beginning of the example game. Notice the piece in the upper right corner (with the X). This is a piece that will connect to your goal. Lacking any other strategy, we decided to try to push it down into position.

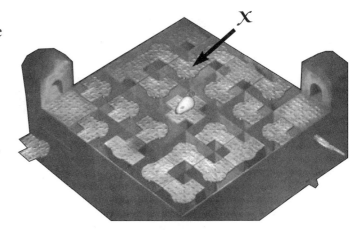

Our first move is at position B (see previous page). This pushes the column down toward our goal.

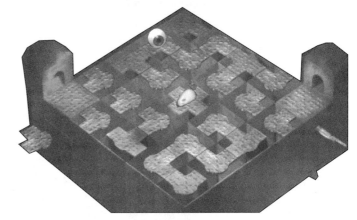

This is the position of the board after the first move. Notice that Stauf has moved the mouse close to his goal. He feels pretty good now.

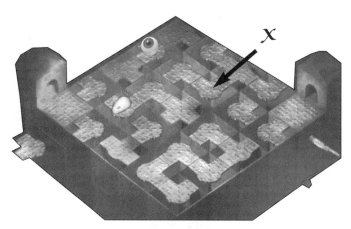

Once again, we moved from position B to try to force the goal piece toward our goal.

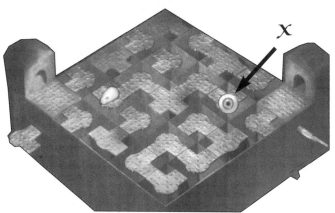

Then we positioned the mouse close to our goal. Notice that the goal piece has moved one space closer to the goal.

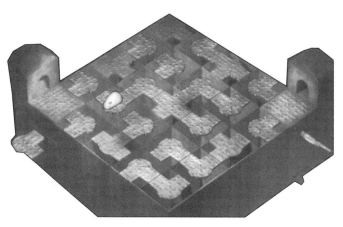

On Stauf's move, he pushed a piece in at position D. He managed to move our goal piece, but there was another like it in the column, so his strategy didn't work. He finished by moving the mouse back close to his goal.

Our final move was to push the piece in again from B, creating a complete path to our goal, winning the game.

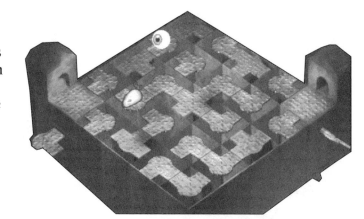

Here is the winning path.

Note: Although we won this game, there was more than a little luck in our victory. Hopefully you'll find this example helpful, even if it isn't a foolproof solution.

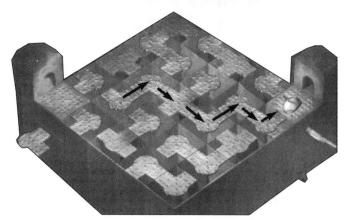

From a different game, here is the winning move. See if you can tell what will happen when the move is made.

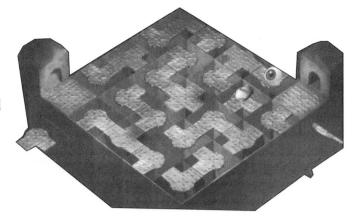

Resetting Solution

There is one other way to approach the Mousetrap Puzzle. It requires that you reset the game, looking for specific starting conditions. If you learn to recognize favorable conditions, however, you can win the game in two moves fairly reliably. The key to this method is realizing that Stauf will always make the move that gets the mouse closest to his goal. In the example below, you'll see how to turn that to your advantage. (See page 241 for puzzle chart.)

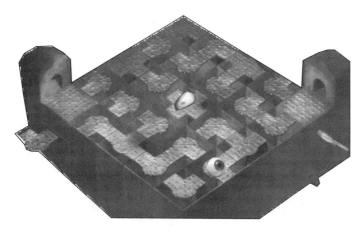

Here is the starting move of the puzzle after it has been reset several times. Notice that a piece is already leading to our goal. Notice also that when we push the outside piece up from position F, Stauf's best move will be at F again. The result of his move is to position the mouse one step closer to his goal (as shown in the lower picture).

Our second move is from position G, which sets up the path to the goal and wins the game. This kind of pattern can occur at any part of the game board, and if you learn to recognize it, you can win every time.

Puzzle #5

Mondrian Painting (Picture Gallery)

Clues

 #1   The object is to choose the last possible space.
 #2   You can't chose a space that is adjacent to a previously chosen space.

Note: The basic trick to this puzzle is to start in one of two places. If you start anywhere else, there is no way to win. The two starting places are shown below, and a sample sequence appears on the next page.

Solution

Start Position 1

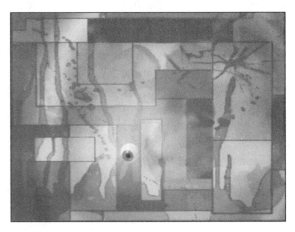

Start Position 2

Mondrian Puzzle Tips

The object of this puzzle is to be the last player to take a turn.

Touching a colored space on the painting turns it to a brightly colored space, and affects any adjacent spaces as well. This constitutes a turn, and after yours is finished, Stauf will choose a space and turn adjacent spaces grey. (You cannot choose spaces that have already been affected.) Because this is an Artifical Intelligence game, there are no specific solutions. It is a different game, every time. There are, however, some strategies that can lead to winning solutions.

- You must begin on one of the two squares shown on the preceeding page to have much chance of winning.

- Notice that some spaces can be left as single "islands" in groups of adjacent spaces. You can use these to your advantage by thinking ahead and leaving them unrestored— but be careful, Stauf is looking for similar opportunities!

Sample Game

In this example, the first move made was on Start Position 1 (see previous page). The four pieces around it have now been restored to bright color. Stauf chooses as his answering turn the rectangle we've marked with the letter X, turning it and the six pieces it touches a dull grey.

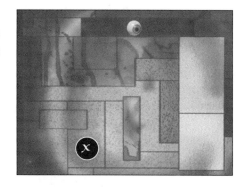

The only winning option is to choose the long black rectangle toward the top of the painting (see the eyeball, top screen); it will restore most of the spaces to a bright color. This will narrow the choices down to two moves—one for Stauf, and the last one for you!

Stauf choses the middle rectangle on the far right, leaving you the final victorious move. In this case, choosing the only remaining rectangle wins the game.

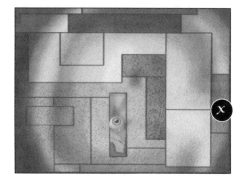

Puzzle #6

Ꮒumber Chain (Gꜳme Ꮢoom)

Clues

   #1   Replace all of the nine white balls with the numbered balls in sequential order.

   #2   There are hidden lines of influence between the balls. Figure out what they are and you can solve this mystery.

Note: It's all in where you start.

Solution

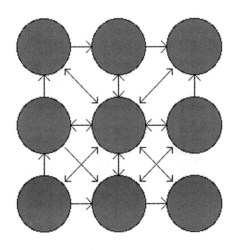

Hidden lines of force and the solution.

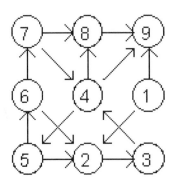

Puzzle #7

Four Spiders (Bathroom)

Clues

#1   Swap the positions of the brown spiders on the top with those of the white spiders on the bottom.

#2   You can move along straight lines only from one point to the next.

#3   It must be done in seven moves.

#4   A move is complete when another spider is selected.

Note: Read that last clue. That's the key to doing it in seven moves.

Solution

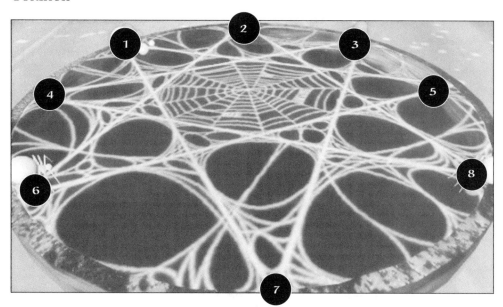

Move 1: 1⇒5
Move 2: 3⇒7⇒1
Move 3: 8⇒4⇒3°7
Move 4: 6⇒2⇒8⇒4⇒3
Move 5: 5⇒6⇒2⇒8
Move 6: 1⇒5⇒6
Move 7: 7⇒1

Puzzle #8

Sliding Mirror (Knox's Room)

Clues

#1 By sliding the individual panes, restore the mirror to its original state.

#2 Use the desilvering sections of the mirror as clues to the solution.

Note: The mirror rotates sideways when you click on it, showing you how it will look when you've solved the puzzle. Paying strict attention to the relationship between the gold bands of color and the dark patches is essential.

Solution

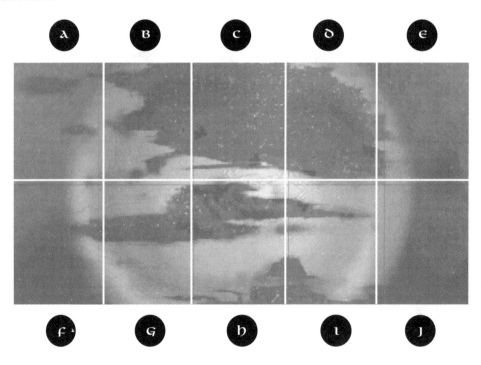

The picture above shows the panels of the mirror in their proper positions. All you have to do is move them until they look like this. To find out how, turn the page.

Mirror Puzzle Strategies

Each time it's started, this puzzle begins in a random configuration. Although the solution itself is relatively simple, it is complicated by the fact that 50% of the time, the game is begun in such a configuration that *it cannot be solved.* Unfortunately, it's impossible to tell if the puzzle can be solved until the last few moves.

General Strategy:

Note: Because the missing pane is randomly selected each time, your puzzle may not match the examples given exactly. The strategy, however, is consistent, and should work every time you're presented with a solveable version of this puzzle. Also note that the ideal solution proceeds from left to right, solving one column at a time.

It is helpful to think of the puzzle as divided into groups of four panes at a time that form a square. These square groups are referred to as cells. We've laid out the puzzle so there are four cells as shown below:

Cell 1

Cell 2

Cell 3

Cell 4

When you rotate a cell, it is implied that one of the panes in the cell must be the empty one. The empty pane is then moved around the cell so that all the pieces change positions.

For example, a clockwise rotation of cell #4 might look like this:

Start

A	B	C	D	E
F	G	H	I	

Move 1

A	B	C	D	
F	G	H	I	E

Move 2

A	B	C		D
F	G	H	I	E

Move 3

A	B	C	I	D
F	G	H		E

Notice how all three letters in the cell were rotated clockwise one position about the center of the cell.

Now let's look at a puzzle example. The first step is to get the letters "A" and "F" into column #1. To do this, follow these steps:

1) Move pane "A" to the lower position in column 1. If pane "F" is in column #1 when "A" is in a position like this:

F		B	H	E
A	G	C	I	D

a) Rotate Cell #1 clockwise so that pane "F" is in Cell #2, but pane "A" is not.

A	F	B	H	E
G		C	I	D

b) Rotate cell #2 clockwise so that pane "F" is no longer in Cell #1.

a		f	h	e
G	c	B	ı	ð

c) Rotate Cell #1 counterclockwise so that pane "A" is back in the lower position of column #1.

	c	f	h	e
a	G	B	ı	ð

2) Move pane "F" so that it is in Cell #2.
3) Rotate Cell #2 until pane "F" is adjacent to pane "A."
4) Rotate Cell #1 clockwise.

Pane "A" should now be in the top of column #1 and pane "F" should be in the bottom of column #1. Column #1 is now finished. Panes "A" and "F" should now be considered frozen for the rest of the puzzle and never moved.

The next step is to solve column #2 by following the four steps detailed above. Just apply these steps to panes "B" and "G," rather than "A" and "F." Once column #2 is solved, you can move on and solve column #3 in the same fashion.

Finally, when column #3 is solved (when panes "C" and "H" are in their final positions), rotate Cell #4 until pane "E" is in the upper right corner. If pane "D" is in the top row, you've solved the puzzle. If pane "I" is in the top row, then the puzzle is unsolvable, and you'll have to reset the puzzle (hopefully getting a solveable one on the next randomization).

Specific Example of Mirror Puzzle

The first order of business is always to rotate the panes around until pane "A" is in the lower left corner.

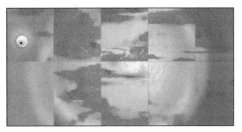

"A" is in the upper left corner.

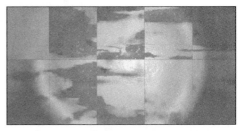

"A" is in the lower left corner.

Now, rotate the panes until "F" is in Cell #2.

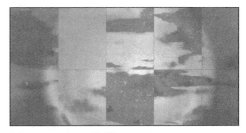

Now rotate Cell #2 counter-clockwise, until pane "F" is adjacent to pane "A."

Rotate Cell #1 clockwise until "A" is in the top left corner, with pane "F" underneath it. Now column #1 is finished, and should be considered frozen throughout the remainder of this puzzle.

The next task is to finish column #2, with "B" on top of pane "G." Rotate Cell #2 around, until "B" is in the top position of column #2. In the picture, pane "B" is about to move from the top of column 3 to the top of column 2.

Column #2 is now finished, and should also be considered frozen.

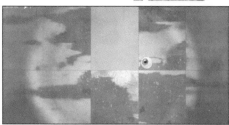

Pane "H" is at the top of column 4, ready to rotate to the top of column 3.

Now, rotate Cell #3 around counterclockwise until pane "H" is in its correct position, with pane "C" above it. And ta-da, that's the end of column #3.

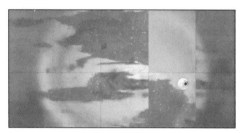

Now, move pane "D" up to the top of column #4.

Now pane "D" is at the top of the column, and the puzzle is almost solved.

Finally, move pane "I" into its correct position in column #4, and the puzzle will complete itself.

Important Note:

Although it was possible to solve this puzzle, some configurations can not be solved, and this strategy will not work every time. Unfortunately, it is difficult to tell if a puzzle can be solved until you have gotten pretty far into it.

Puzzle #9

Centaur (Griphon) Puzzle (Chapel)

Clues

#1   You're playing against Stauf.
#2   To win, be the first to create an unbroken path that touches all three sides of the triangular field.
#3   A corner hexagon counts as touching two sides at once.

Note: This is one of the easiest challenges you'll find in Stauf's Mansion, if you know where to make your first move!

Solution

Always start in the center of the triangle. Stauf will try to block you in one direction or the other. Move opposite his block and start building a path toward the nearest corner. Connecting to a corner automatically connects two sides. Watch for Stauf's attempts to prevent you from reaching the third side, though. If you notice he is building little traps, start working toward the third side and come back to the corner when you've beaten the trap. Once you reach a certain point in this puzzle, Stauf appears to give up and the rest is a cruise.

All three of the games shown above are one move away from a win. All three started in the middle and worked toward a corner. Notice that Stauf successfully blocked the corner route in the game shown on the right, but he couldn't prevent the path from reaching all three sides.

It is possible to win by starting at one of the corners and heading toward the third side, but it is trickier and you have to counter Stauf's moves. For variety, you might try that approach, however.

Puzzle #10

Railroad Switcher (Attic)

Clues
- #1   Manipulate the cars by switching between the top and the bottom track. Use the switcher.
- #2   The letters will spell out "Stauf."

Note: This puzzle is not too difficult, but it does take a while. Be sure to keep track of your time. . .

Solution

First, click on the left-hand switch, then move the letter "A" down and around until it ends up to the left of the "F."

Repeat this procedure with letters "U" and the "S."

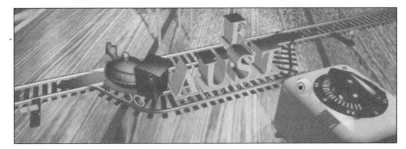

Move the "T," then the "S," the "U," and "A" to the bottom track.

Move the "F" to the far right on the top track.

Now move the "A" to the top track to the left of the "F."
Move the "U" to the mid-point of the upper track, then move
the "S" to the left of the "U" and the "T" to the left of the "S."

Move the "A" to the bottom track, followed by the "T" and the "S." Move the "U" to the left side of the "F."

Move the "S" from the bottom track to the mid-point of the upper track.
Move the "T" from the bottom track to the left side of the "S."
Move the "A" from the bottom track to the left side of the "U."

Move the "T" down and around so it's on the left side of the "A." Use the bottom track.
Push the "S" to the right against the "T" on the top track. That's it!

Puzzle #11

Ten Plates Stacked on a Star (Kitchen)

Clues
- #1 The object is to create five stacks of two plates on every point of the star pattern.
- #2 A plate must jump two plates, stacked or not.
- #3 Once moved, a plate cannot be moved again.

Note: Remember, jumping two plates, stacked or not—a plate can move several positions, but it must jump over two plates during the move.

Solution

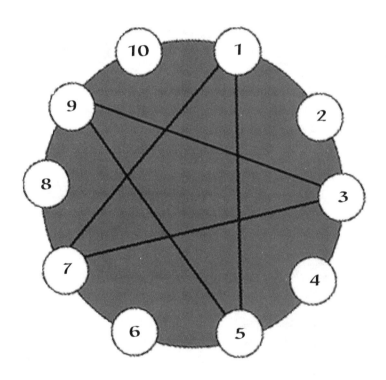

Move 1: 8⇒1

Move 2: 6⇒3

Move 3: 10⇒5

Move 4: 4⇒7

Move 5: 2⇒9

Puzzle #12

Dice Puzzle (Temple's Room)

Clues

#1 You have to make a path from the starting die face to the ending one at the opposite side of the cube.

#2 The number of pips don't stand for numbers, they indicate direction.

#3 The direction you choose defines the meaning of the die face from which you move.

Note: The object is to create a path from the bottom left corner to the upper right corner by clicking on the faces of the stacked dice. The first time you click on a die face of a particular number, then click on another die face, you set the direction for the first number. After that, if you click on that number again, the path will automatically move in the direction you used the first time. Just remember, the direction set is the direction you moved *from*. For instance, if you click on the face with the 4 to the right of the start point, then click on the 4 above that one, the path will automatically move up to the face with the 2 above the second 4. If that doesn't make sense, try it for yourself.

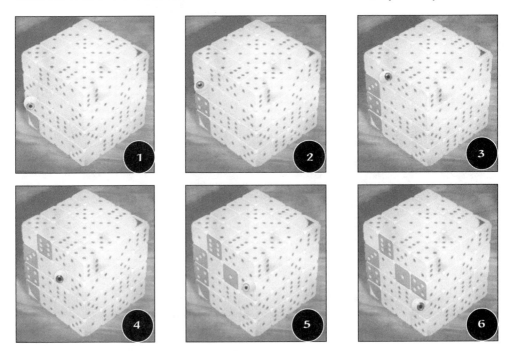

Alternate Solution 1

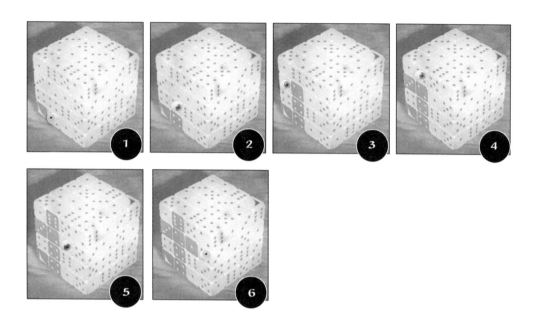

Alternate Solution 2

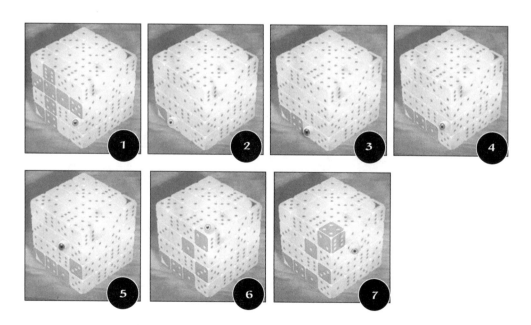

Puzzle #13

Word Labyrinth (Burden's Room)

Clues

#1   You must reveal two fifteen letter words.

#2   Once a letter has been chosen, you may not pass through
      that letter's space again.

#3   The outer corridor remains open.

Note: This puzzle is pretty easy. Just be sure to keep the paths open and
try to plan ahead once you've figured out the words in the puzzle.
Remember, the outer corridor is always open, so you can use it to get to
any letter on the outer edge of the labyrinth. Try to plan your paths
through the center of the labyrinth carefully so you don't lock yourself in.

Solution

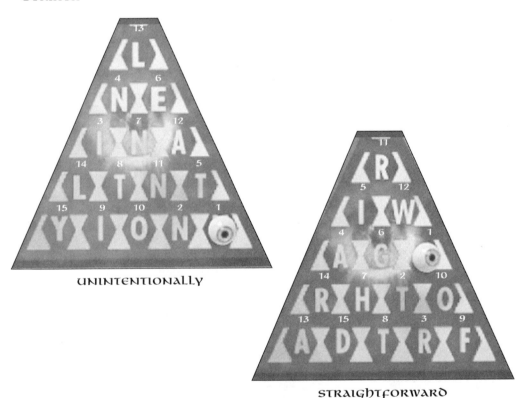

UNINTENTIONALLY

STRAIGHTFORWARD

Puzzle #14

Necklace (Heine's Room)

Clues

#1   Each gem must be adjacent to a gem of a matching color.

#2   You can rotate a cluster of gems or swap positions with
        another cluster.

Note: This puzzle can seem pretty confusing, and there's probably more
than one way to solve it.

Solution

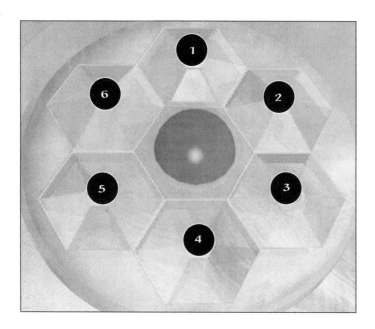

Swap #3 & #4
Swap #3 & #6
Swap #3 & #5

Turn #6 twice
Turn #5 twice
Turn #4 five times
Turn #3 four times
Turn #2 twice

Puzzle #15

Blood and Honey (Room at the Top)

Clues

#1   You're playing against Stauf.
#2   Try to end with more honey in the comb than blood.
#3   Globules divide in two when moved to an adjacent cell.
     But jumping the maximum of two cells moves the globule.
#4   Honey absorbes adjacent cells filled with blood and vice versa.

Note: This may be the most challenging puzzle that Stauf will throw at you. Strategies for playing are difficult to devise, and sometimes seem to require intuition more than specific knowledge. However, one very useful technique to use while learning how to play is having Samantha make the next move. You can have Samantha make as many moves as you want, and she'll play Stauf a tough game. Below, we show an example of a game played entirely by Samantha. It illustrates some of the strategies used in this game.

General Notes:

- Stauf tends to respond the way he's treated; i.e., if you jump two spaces to take over a number of his cells, he'll retaliate if he can. If you play defensively, so will he (for the most part).

- Try to think ahead at least a move, especially when engaging in direct cell-to-cell combat with Stauf. The strongest tactic you can use is trading for more pieces than you're giving up.

- Patience is a key to winning. Even though situations often look bleak, as though Stauf has the full advantage, the tides do turn, if only one cell at a time.

- There are 60 cells in total. You need to make 31 of them yellow in order to win.

Note: Count pieces carefully! Even when Honey has more pieces on the board than Blood does, it often looks as though Blood is winning (because red is a stronger color than yellow).

Opening Moves of a Winning Game

After Honey's initial move, and Blood's response, Honey must jump and begin a skirmish with Blood, even though Honey will lose any apparent advantage when Blood absorbs all of Honey's cells in that little battle. Honey now needs to absorb Blood's cell at the very top by another two-space jump.

Note: *Pictures have been modified to show occupied cells more clearly.*

Blood will play more defensively now.

Honey must take a protective stance.

Blood gets more daring, almost baiting Honey to jump. That wouldn't be too wise, though.

Honey needs to continue playing defensively. Blood reciprocates.

Honey plays at the top—at the eyeball—while Blood gets aggressive at the bottom, absorbing Honey's lone cell.

Honey moves defensively—at eyeball—and Blood behaves defensively, too.

Honey continues on a defensive path and Blood plays along.

Honey is in consolidating mode. Blood is circling up toward Honey's cells, on the left.

Time for Honey to be aggressive.

Blood tries to prevent Honey from interfering on the left.

Honey must jump to this cell and intimidate Blood's hold.

Blood absorbs some of honey's cells, although taking a defensive move by filling in the hexagonal circle.

Although Blood has three more pieces on the board at this point than Honey, this is a winable situation for Honey. It is just a matter of patience and perseverance. The pictures on the next page illustrate the general trends of the rest of the game. The last picture shows Honey winning.

Blood and Honey is about gaining and losing every step of the way. Sometimes it will seem as if you're losing ground, but hang in there.

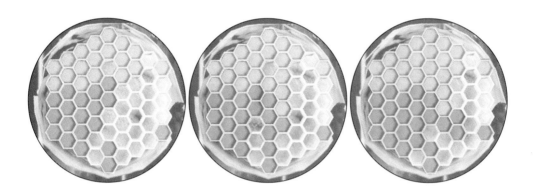

Even toward the end, it's touch and go, but Honey prevails with the last move.

Honey Wins!

Puzzle #16

Moving House (Music Room)

Clues
- #1   Move the pieces around until you can move the piano off
the board.
- #2   This one's difficult.

Note: Well, that's about the size of it. This one is very difficult, and by our best estimate, it requires at least 90 moves to complete. You'll see all the moves below, with pictures approximately every ten moves.

Solution

Starting position

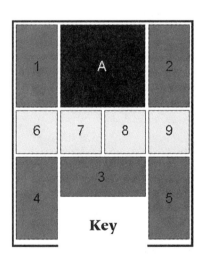

Key

Moves 1-10:

3⇓, 7⇓ ⇒, 6⇒ ⇓, 4⇑, 3⇐, 7⇓, 6⇒, 4⇒

Moves 11-20:

1⇓ ⇓, A⇐, 8 ⇑ ⇑, 6⇑ ⇑, 7⇑ ⇑, 5⇐

Moves 21-30:

9⇓ ⇓, 2⇓ ⇓, 8⇒, 6⇒, A⇒, 1⇑ ⇑, 4⇐

Moves 31-41:

7⇐ ⇓, A⇓, 8⇐ ⇐, 6⇑ ⇐, 2⇑ ⇑, 9⇑ ⇑

Moves 42-51:

5⇒, 7⇒ ⇓, A⇓, 8⇓ ⇒, 1⇒, 4⇑ ⇑, A⇐

Moves 52-61:

9⇐ ⇓, 5⇑, 7⇒, 9⇓, A⇒, 4⇓ ⇓, 1⇐, 6⇐

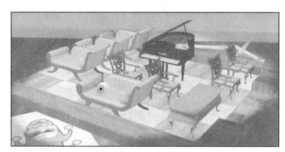

Moves 62-71:

8⇐, 2⇐, 5⇑ ⇑, A⇒, 8⇓ ⇓, 6 ⇓ ⇓, 1⇒

Moves 72-81:

4⇑ ⇑, 8⇐ ⇑, 3⇑, 9⇐ ⇐, 7⇐ ⇐, A⇓

Moves 82-90:

6⇒ ⇒, 8⇒ ⇒, 3⇑, 7⇑⇐, A⇐ ⇓

Puzzle #17

Trilobite (Dining Room)

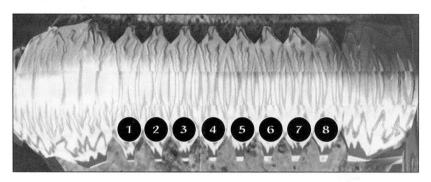

Clues

#1 You're playing against Stauf.

#2 Get four of your bon bons in a row before Stauf does.

#3 Drop a new bon bon onto a stack by selecting a vertical section of the trilobite.

#4 The bon bons can be connected vertically, horizontally or diagonally.

#5 Watch out for those diagonal connections. They can be hard to see.

Note: Stauf is a wily opponent. He'll build in several directions and trap you if you're not very careful. However, we have come up with one reliable strategy, but it depends on what move Stauf makes first. . . .

Solution

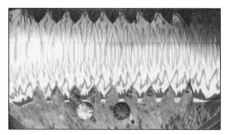 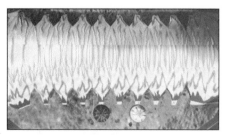

Your first move should be in column 3 or column 6. For these strategies to work, Stauf must then move two columns away (in column 5 or column 4) as shown. On the next page, you'll see completed games using this starting strategy.

| Remember, your first move is 1. |
| All odd-numbered moves are yours. |

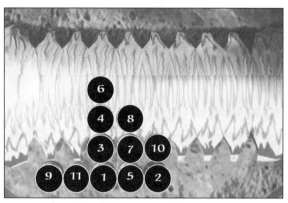

This is the shortest solution we've found, with a win on the 11th move! At move 9, Stauf makes a major mistake, completely missing the fact that you will make four along the bottom on the next move.

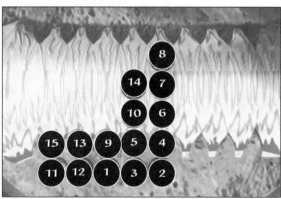

This solution starts out like the one above, but your second move is in column 4. You keep setting up for four-in-a-row along the bottom left and Stauf gets unlucky after move 13!

In the game shown below, Stauf attempts a trap at move 6. If you don't block with move 7, he'll get an open three and you'll lose. However, at your

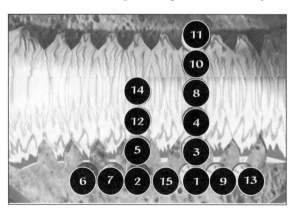

move 9, he doesn't recognize the potential threat and builds his three-in-a-row on column 6, which you block. His move 12 still ignores your trap, which you spring on move 13. If he blocks your three, you'll create an open three on the next move. Either way Stauf loses. He takes the easy way out and lets you win with move 15.

Puzzle #18

Switchboard (Doll Room)

Clues

#1 Interchange the white bishops on one side with the black bishops on the other.

#2 You can move any piece in any order, but it must move along a straight line, and not land in line with a bishop of the opposite color.

#3 I think I can do it in 18 moves.

Notes: This puzzle can get tricky if you try to solve it by brute force. On the other hand, you might want to give it a try before using Samantha's eighteen-move answer listed on these pages.

Solution

Move 1: 10⇒7

Move 2: 1⇒8

Move 3: 2⇒3

Move 4: 7⇒4

Move 5: 3⇒5

Move 6: 8⇒10

Move 7: 9⇒6

Move 8: 6⇒1

Move 9: 4⇒6

Move 10: 5⇒2

Move 11: 10⇒5

Move 12: 6⇒8

Move 13: 5⇒7

Move 14: 2⇒4

Move 15: 8⇒3

Move 16: 7⇒10

Move 17: 4⇒9

Move 18: 3⇒2

Puzzle #19

Pente (Doll House)

Clues

  #1   You're playing against Stauf.
  #2   Get five of your pieces in a row, or capture five (pairs) of your opponent's pieces to win.
  #3   Try not to let Stauf get four unchecked pieces in a row or else you are doomed.

Notes: Pente players will rejoice to find a familiar game. However, for those players unfamiliar with Pente, here are some basics strategies. Stauf can be beaten, but this is the only game that Samantha cannot complete. Therefore, you'll need your wits about you to defeat Stauf. If at first you don't succeed. . . Well, Stauf will let you try again. And again. . . .

General Strategies

Captured Pairs

One added twist in Pente is that players can "capture" opponents' pieces by enclosing a pair of connected pieces like so:

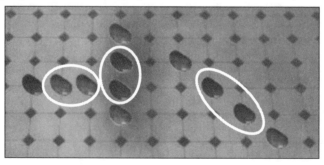

and then remove the two captured pieces. It is also possible, though rare, to make double captures as shown below. (X takes the pieces.)

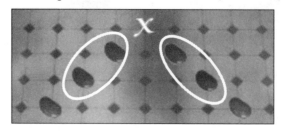

You must reach an "open four," that is, four connected pieces of your color without one of Stauf's on either end of the line of four. Once you achieve an open four, you've won the game.

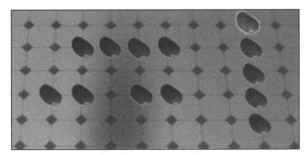

Examples of open fours (left) and closed four (right)

Open threes are dangerous, because they can lead to open fours. Prevent open fours by making sure to put one of your pieces on one end of an open three.

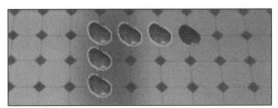

Examples of open and closed threes

It is possible to force wins by a using a combination of open threes and captured pairs. For instance, the more captured pairs you have taken, the more limited your opponent's options will be.

The more pieces you have on the board, the better. In general, it's a wise idea to avoid captures unless there is a reciprocal capture available.

A good general strategy (and stalling device) is to add a fourth piece onto closed threes. Although it seems unimportant, this simple move often opens up more available formations.

Special Note: The first time you play Stauf at Pente, you get the first move—a definite advantage. If you then replay the game to try for a second ending, Stauf will get the first move the next game. If you persist, playing for a third ending (having already beaten Stauf twice), Stauf will play a very tough game, looking five moves ahead. Don't say we didn't warn you. (Strategies shown here were for the first time through only!)

Sample Game

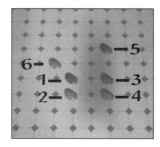 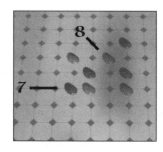 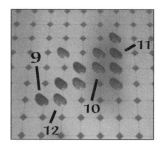

Move 1-4: Always begin as close to the center as possible. Not only is this traditional Pente form, but it gives you more options as well.

Move 5: Building triangular forms using alternating spaces helps.

Move 7: Moving here prevents Stauf from having an open three on his next move, and sets up a potential four-in-a-row as well.

Move 8: Stauf blocks red's potential open four, and threatens to capture the two diagonal pieces. Go ahead and block the threat.

Move 13: Stauf's setting up potential open threes everywhere. Don't let him! In fact, this move threatens to jump his two pieces.

Move 14: Stauf uses the tactic of adding a fourth piece onto a closed three—stalling for time, and hoping that you don't see that he has a potential win. Block him with move 15.

Move 17: Jumping Stauf's pair means that red comes out ahead.

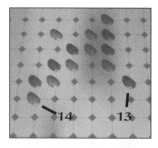 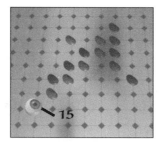 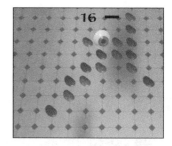

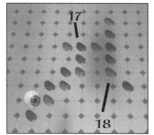

Move 19: Now add that fourth piece to the closed three.

Move 21: Avoid the potential capture.

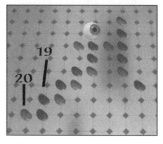

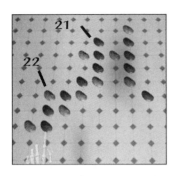
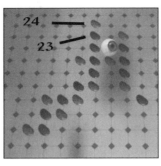
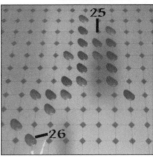

Move 22-23: Stauf threatens another capture here—ignore it for the moment and add a fourth to the closed three.

Move 25: Go for the open three.

Move 26-27: Stauf jumped red's pieces. Keep on building an open four!

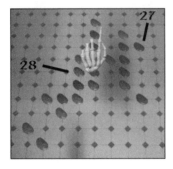

Move 28-29: Stauf captures a pair, breaking up red's open four. Ha. Ignore his insignificant gesture, and rebuild that open four.

Move 30-31: He'll only get one more pair before red wins the game. Just get right back in there and recreate the open four.

Move 32-33: Stauf tries to divert red's attention by building his own open four. It really doesn't matter. This game is red's. Stauf loses!

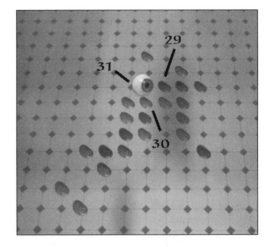

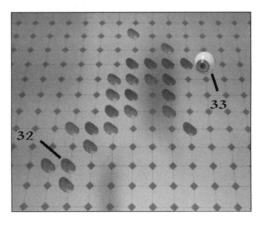

THE INTERVIEW WITH GRAEME & ROB

Rusel—How did you come to do *The 11th Hour*? With the success of *The 7th Guest*, you must have been on top of the world.

Graeme—Ahuh ahuh ahuh ahuh ahuh.

Rusel—So you didn't have to do it?

Graeme—Uh, no. I didn't really want to do it. I mean, Rob wanted to do it. Towards the end of *The 7th Guest*, which was in some ways a fiasco, we were *really* cool. But we were broke.

[laughter]

Alex—So you had to do it to get a contract going.

Graeme—Yeah, we had two contracts, one was up for a game called *Cybernet*. The other one was for a game called *The 11th Hour*, based upon Stauf, but years later. We already had most of the files inside the box. Or so we thought. Cybernet—we

283

decided we didn't want to give that to Virgin; it was too good a game design. We still haven't done it. And *The 11th Hour*, you know, was a natural product for them, so it was to be a "quick" sequel.

Rusel—So, it's a quick sequel?

Graeme—(ironic laugh): Yeah, right, three years later. Just about done.

Rusel—So, *Cybernet*, is that something you're *going* to do?

Graeme—No, I doubt whether we'll ever do that one, now—kinda moved on from the way we designed games and a lot of the interactivity we presented through them. I learned a lot from *The 11th Hour*, like how to expand on stories and make a story interactive. *The 11th Hour*'s very faithful to *The 7th Guest*, but it was a learning experience for us as well.

Rusel—What are some of the things you want to do now that you learned from that?

Graeme—I've learned perhaps most of all that I want to be, need to be, a storyteller, and that means that I want it to be my story—have my start, my middle, my end—rather than allow the stories to be so interactive that there's a zillion endings, a billion middles, and hundred beginnings. If you can do one good story, one really great story, that outweighs having a hundred weak stories.

Rusel—How does the interactive part of it come in? How is that different from a movie, or a novel?

Graeme—Well, I think, more interesting is offering character-based interactivity. If you looked at *Alien*—your view in *Alien* is like the view of Ripley—the good person. But, if you had gone from Ashley's point of view, then gosh, that would be a different movie. Then Ripley would be the annoying, good person and you'd think, "Why in the hell did you try all this for?" If you could see the movie from the alien's point of view, like "Gosh, where's dinner?" You see three completely different stories, but exactly the same sequence of events.

Rusel—Which has been done in literature very well. Have you ever seen Kurasawa's movie *Rashoman*?

Graeme—Yes. *Rashoman*, yes. That's a very good example. Having that—that is an interactive story for me.

Rusel—But still if the story is relatively fixed in terms of events, then what's the reward for the player other than "this is the POV"?

Graeme—Oh, to learn more about the characters, offering deeper interest in some of the characters, so you can go explore more of what their motives are within their current environment and more who they are, and perhaps see more into why they are taking the actions they are taking.

Rusel—Is that the idea behind your upcoming product, *Tender Loving Care?*

Graeme—To a certain degree. That's Rob's product. It's not mine. We tend to have different thoughts . . .

Rusel—Do you have a product that you're working on now, besides *11th Hour*?

Graeme—No. For a while I did, but right now I want to take some time off; it's been way-the-heck too busy. . . Though I DO want to do to the American public what Orson Welles did to the American public with the *War of the Worlds* broadcast.

[laughter]

Graeme—Otherwise, you're out with multimedia. Scare them so much into thinking that something's going on, so they actually rush out and build a bunker in their backyard.

Rusel—You want to have a big effect.

Graeme—On each individual, yeah.

Rusel—When you finished *The 7th Guest*, and you said you didn't want to do *The 11th Hour* at the time, what was in your mind to do at that point? Did you want to take a break or did you want to do another game immediately? What was that your thinking at the time?

Graeme—What we were thinking at the time was that survival was the main issue. Virgin had paid us no money at the end of *The 7th Guest*. We thought we were only going to sell like 60,000 units—the game might come and go. We were just glad to get *7th Guest* out.

Rusel—So how many units did you sell so far? Do you know?

Graeme—Just over 1.5 million.

Rusel—More than 60,000!

Graeme—More than 60,000. Yes. That's quite a bit.

Rusel—So how does that change things? Obviously, now you have a really successful product and now you don't expect to sell 50,000 of *The 11th Hour*. You know you're going out the door with 300,000.

Graeme—Oh, we'll sell at least 70,000.

Rusel—At least.

Rusel—So how does that affect your thinking? Obviously, now you're in the playground. You can do much more of what you want. You've got a track record and all that stuff, so, what's your feeling now? How's it been since you've reached that point of "now we're successful, we know it"? What are the issues that come up for you there?

Graeme—Proving that Trilobyte's not a one-hit wonder; adding stability to our software schedules—I guess more like taking the company to the next level. We've got so much going on now. Besides *11th Hour*, we've got *Dog Eat Dog, Clandestiny, Tender Loving Care*—that's three, all in production, and going from being a one-hit, one product producer to a multiple product publisher—it's the big transition.

Rusel—How much are you personally involved in the transition to publisher?

Graeme—I think the management of the company is going to become my major interest.

Rusel—Is that satisfying to you?

Graeme—Oh yeah. Jesus, forty-five people come in here every day, now. We have to look after them. Those people make the product. Those people are the most important people this company has. It's just a company made up by, you know, people who come in each day.

Rusel—It's kind of ironic in a way that somebody who has created and innovated as you have becomes a manager type. Do you feel now that you can actually have more of your own creative ideas realized simply because there are all these other people working and doing more than you could possibly do alone?

Graeme—To a certain extent. Every ten days more than a man-year goes past here. It's just incredible. . . every ten days. And that's just the kind of work that goes on here, now. I think what it allows is that a lot of the initial implementation of, say, technology or design is still going to come from Rob and me, but the actual cool implementation, taking it to final, won't necessarily be from us.

Alex—Do you think that this will be enough for you for a while, managing your company and taking sort of a back seat with the creative stuff, or are you going to wake up a year from now and say, "God what have I been doing?"

Graeme—Yeah, but I think it's that time. I just spent the last six years of my life doing nothing but this. I have a baby daughter. I want to sit back and do something a little bit less stressful, and cut back on the hours a little bit. I want to watch my daughter grow up and learn to talk and actually know who I am. Instead of, "Oh, yeah, you're the guy that I come to see sometimes in the office, yeah! I remember you!"

Rusel—How old is she now?

Graeme—Seven months.

Rusel—It's all pretty magical.

Graeme—It's pretty amazing.

Rob enters the room, but quickly passes out the door again, with a wink.

Graeme—Rob is going to go get some coffee, I bet.

Graeme—There she is.

[Admiring baby pictures of Graeme's gorgeous baby daughter.]

Alex—Oh, she's beautiful, that face . . . she looks like you.

Graeme—(a bark of hysterical laughter) Seven months is a little bit early to tell? Yeah, the beard's isn't quite there yet—the hair's not there yet, either! She's pretty bald.

Alex—She looks like a really happy baby, too.

Graeme—Yes, she is.

Rusel—We heard about your shower. . . someday I've got to see this.

[Graeme's computer-controlled shower is a subject of discussion around Trilobyte.]

Graeme—Oh, the *Star Trek* shower?

Rusel—Yeah, the computerized shower.

Graeme—I don't trust it!

Rusel—That was my first thought too, but I'm pretty curious.

Graeme—Yeah, there's something more trustworthy about an analog device.

[Rob at this point shows up looking distracted, as if his mind is on other things. He sits in a chair and holds his coffee mug in two hands. We adjust the microphone and continue the interview.

Rusel—Nice of you to join us, Rob.

Rob—(after a moment of deep thought) Oh, yeah. . . *right!*

Alex—Drink that coffee, Rob!

Rusel—After a couple days immersed in *11th Hour*, anything amuses us —we're beyond personal thought now.

Graeme—We'll have to put that down in the thing, "after a couple of days of playing, you may experience irrational thoughts . . ."

Alex—Put it on the box, as a warning.

Graeme—Exactly, it's actually interesting after the ending.

Alex—Do not operate heavy machinery . . .

Rusel—And now, we are joined by Rob Landeros, a key figure in this whole experience. . . We were talking about a couple of things, like what happened at the end of *7th Guest* and how you got into this—

Graeme—Like *Cybernet* and *11th Hour*. How *Cybernet* was too good for Virgin, so we gave them *11th Hour*—

Rob—You DIDN'T tell them that, didja!? Actually, I could give a shit. . .

[Raucous laughter]

Rob—We had such a great design!

Graeme—Well, we thought it was. Of course, now it's probably obsolete. . .

Rusel—Yeah, now everything's Cyber this and Cyber that.

Graeme—Well, if we finished it up right now, and released it this summer, it'd have been right on time! We were three years ahead of ourselves, you see.

Rusel—Well, as usual, right? Weren't you way ahead of yourselves with *The 7th Guest*, too?

Rob—Oh, we're ahead of ourselves—in fact, we have to catch up with ourselves! It's a tough job. Maybe if we slow down, we'll give ourselves the chance to catch up.

Alex—There's something I wanted to ask about *The 11th Hour*, which is about the overall form of it. I mean, *7th Guest* is kinda sorta linear, yet kind of vague at the same time. It's hard to tell exactly what's going on in the story line until you get more and more into it but now it's—

Graeme—That was on purpose.

Alex—Yeah, which I really like.

Graeme— But it wasn't a commercial decision designed to sell more products!

Alex—I don't care. I like it. I thought it was like throwing yourself into the unknown and just being out there. But you know, Johnny Consumer maybe didn't care for that. . . though they're still buying it!

Graeme—Wasn't a concern. . .

Rusel—These are problems we all should have.

Alex—But, what I'm wondering is—the thing that's interesting having seen *7th Guest* and now having seen *The 11th Hour*—is that there really is an overall structure and a form, and what interests me is how you made decisions to weave in the different story elements and pieces—like, "how much do you tell?" It works really well. The pacing between the video clips and how much you're given, and then all of a sudden you're treasure hunting in between—it's really slick. How did you go about determining where these different elements come in? Did it come out the way you expected it to?

[Laughter from Rob and Graeme]

[Silence]

[More silence]

Rob—I'm trying to remember—after all, it's been almost three years since I worked through these issues.

Graeme—Well, actually the way he came up with the cut list, was, Rob just took a video cassette home one night and then didn't sleep for two days, and two days later comes in with this piece of paper with all these numbers on it. He said, "There you go." Do you remember that?

Rob—Uh . . .

Graeme—You and that VHS videocassette? Four pages with all these numbers, and written under them...

Rob—Right, I went through all the video to define the scenes by timecode numbers. But before that, I had already identified elements within the movie that would lend themselves thematically to objects that might be found in the mansion.

Graeme—I thought those were the clip sizes, too, for the secret clips.

Rob—Oh, right, yeah, that's true. . . I isolated the little teaser clips that show just enough of a particular scene to be intriguing. Well, for example, the razor blade. . . that was a treasure hunt item. If you actually look at the video with it, it's a scene where Marie holds a razor blade up to Chuck's throat. We isolated that scene and tried to envision the effect it would have if you saw that little clip all by itself. We saw it as the kind of thing you'd see in a film trailer or something used as a teaser. Kind of dramatic, with the razor blade. So what happens when you find the razor blade in answer to treasure hunt riddle, is that the player sees the scene out of context and it creates a mystery—What was that scene all about? This technique also provides a connection between the interactive house and the on-going story.

Rusel—How many hours of film did you actually have to work through?

Rob—I worked with the final edit—60 minutes of video. And so, we just kind of looked at the clips for their interest, in and of themselves, and tried to isolate parts of the video and tie them to something in the house. The requirements of the treasure hunts did not affect the edit of the movie. I wouldn't want to mess with the well-balanced story. I let the story suggest the interactive elements.

Rusel—You obviously wrote what you did in *7th Guest* and said, "Okay, now we want to keep what's good here and we want to improve on it." So, what were you thinking about at that point and how did you implement those ideas, those improvements, into *The 11th Hour* while keeping the spirit of *7th Guest?*

Rob—Well, I guess the first consideration was, I wanted to keep the puzzles. And things start there. And the house! We said "Hey, we built this damn house, it cost us a fortune to build it, we could have built the real one for the same amount of money, and lived in it, or half of it, or something—"

Graeme—We did actually work it out that it would have been cheaper to build the actual house, than render the 3-D house! Although it's interesting that we've since caught that from every other game publisher on the planet, who now seems convinced that the only way to get video in the front is on blue screen and then put computer graphics in the background.

Rusel—Right. The copycat syndrome.

Graeme—Great.

[Ironic laugh from all]

Rusel—But of course, you're not necessarily doing that at all anymore.

Graeme—No.

Rob—Well, if we were going to re-use this virtual set and video.

Graeme—You're going to be cheap and quick.

Rob—Cheap and quick. Then, of course, we had to consider the fact that players of *The 7th Guest* would already be very familiar with the house and navigating about, so I came up with this idea of the treasure hunts to keep it fresh for them and to provide a good reason for exploration. We also strengthened the storyline, characterization, and plot.

Rusel—My question also is, you obviously made changes in the pacing and the overall design interface. In other words, the player is really playing a different kind of game right now. There are a lot of differences that I can identify; for instance, you know who you are. You know why you're there. You've got a very different kind of interface from the Ouija board. You've now got a fairly interactive thing—this game book—it's actually part of the game. To me, these are all significant changes and I'm just interested in how you came up with them.

Rob—Well, a lot of it has to do with POV. In *The 7th Guest*, it's like a kind of a sophomoric approach to film-making—point of view is a camera-mounted-on-the-head kind of thing. It was good, you know, it was the first of its kind, was supposed to be totally immersive, part of the mystery of the "Who am I?" kind of thing, so you never see yourself. You can't tell a really good story from just a camera on a head. A lot of that came from how you tell these stories . . . It became apparent that the story wasn't really coming through. We wanted to correct that situation, so in the process of bolstering up the story and honing it really well, this point of view issue became the thing. Like, you're Carl Denning, but you get to see yourself, just like you did in movies and any other visual art forms. We did a lot with that.

Rusel—What about the GameBook itself and how it interfaces with the game? Was that in from the beginning or was that added in after the design?

Graeme—Well the GameBook was always there, part of the design. Initially all the videos were going to be played back in the GameBook. That was part of the reason why the GameBook has more windows than the main game; it was a way of presenting video, and obviously the video clips and things like that. There's also two game books, a Stauf GameBook and the player GameBook. Actually, Stauf's GameBook you do actually get to see still, in the very beginning of the game. You know, that thing that plays back, it's kind of hokey, the brown GameBook, that's been all covered in mud and stuff? The video was going to play back in there throughout the game as well, but we quickly abandoned that idea. A lot of the interface issues, Rob worked out a fairly clear design of how the GameBook was going to work. And, once that was up and working, well, it's been an ongoing interface issue ever since then.

Rusel—It's like some guy in a movie, you know, this product. . .

Graeme—A GameBook product. Yeah, the GameBook, we were first going to ship that as a separate computer!

Rob—Well, I think the idea was how did we want the house to respond? And then we talked about the player's recording of things, and it's just about how you get information. At one point, we considered having the player find audio and video tapes, and other media in the house that would provide the clues and other information. The GameBook idea was a way to offer hints, too, instead of the Library.

Graeme—A lot of people felt that the fact that we did the Library—even though that was the first game to really offer hints throughout the game—it was a hassle, man!

Rob—I guess they'd rather call the hint lines, you know.

Graeme—Yeah, they'd rather open the hint book up!

[Laughter all around]

Rob—Silly idea. Who'd have thought of something like that?

Rusel—Who wrote the actual hints in *11th Hour*? Various people?

Rob—No, I think I wrote most of it, the clues and hints and all. . . some of them I came across in puzzle books.

Rusel—There's some pretty weird stuff in there.

Alex—Yeah, those anagrams are intense!

Graeme—All of that has come from the main design, though, a sort of consistent feel throughout.

Rusel—They were interesting. Some of them we got pretty quickly and some of them we were, like, clueless. And some of the clueless ones I found clever, and when I discovered the answer I enjoyed it. It's sort of a game within a game. I'm curious what happens when the game comes out. How many people will use the solve function simply to see what's going on in the game and then maybe, in the open house, go back and play the actual puzzles for the fun of it?

The GameBook helps. It offers an easy way to get past difficult puzzles, easier than the Library book. The Library was interesting because, first of all it was pretty obscure, so you wouldn't always know about it. Not at first, anyway. And, secondly, it was a little bit more trouble, and you would think twice before using it to solve a puzzle. You might say, "Well, I know I could go to the Library, but maybe I'll try the puzzle one more time instead of going all the way back to the Library for a hint or solution." Now it's more like, "Hmm, well, if I don't really want to do this, I'll just go into the GameBook. . ."

Rob—The other thing in *7th Guest*, they were afraid they were going to miss out on something, like a video. 'Cause we actually intimated that they would, in the manual!

Rusel—And, of course, it wasn't true at all.

Graeme—Yeah, it was great! That's the best thing we did.

[Hysterical laughter]

Rob—Which was good.

Graeme—So they'd feel all guilty if they skipped to the Library, as if they'd miss the video!

Rusel—Just from my point of view, I think it would be cool if players did miss something if a puzzle was solved for them. I mean, other than the satisfaction of solving it—but some of those games are hard. And, people are different and they have different skills, too. They'll get through some of the games, but some of the AI games are pretty hard to beat.

Graeme—Yeah, I think that it's one of the things about *11th Hour*; there are so many things that appeal to different people, to different game-playing styles. They want to see the story. "I don't want to play these puzzles, though, I just want to play the whole puzzle of the game. . ."

Rob—Of course, you don't necessarily want to leave out crucial points of the story; otherwise, it might not make too much sense. We could have penalized the player for cheating a little bit by keeping some of the extra fun stuff from appearing. But generally, we don't want to frustrate or cheat the audience. We want them to have fun.

Rusel—Even the hints are fun. It's fun to figure out what you're getting at, so, it works on several levels at once.

Rob—Getting back to the GameBook, I've found an answer on that, that there's also a point where, okay, suddenly it's years later and Stauf has kind of entered into the Electronic Age. . .

Alex—He's gone digital.

Rob—Yeah. I've always identified with Stauf in the sense that he's making games, toys for kids of all ages and now it's the 90s, you know. It's easy to do if you're at it, making game machines. . .

Graeme—And you've just gotten a Newton! Ahem, ahem.

[laughter]

Alex—Is he going to design your next title? The computer melts into your hand. . .

Rob—Oh, Stauf.

Graeme—What does Stauf do next, yeah?

Alex—I think, a game show. A realistic game show.

Rob—That's actually pretty close.

Rusel—We heard some rumors here . . .

Graeme—In *The 7th Guest III* we don't really want to do, you know, seventy more years in the future, or anything like that. The premise of *11th Hour* is, what happens if you win *7th Guest?* The premise of *7th Guest III* is, what happens if you lost *The 7th Guest?* It'd be pretty advanced if you'd lost *7th Guest,* you know, dark and fatal. . .

Alex—Oh, nice.

Graeme—You'd finally get to offer, this spiral down the dark. . .

Alex—More dementia.

Rusel—And, a little more mad.

Graeme—Will the tunnel ever stop?

[Burst of demented laughter]

Alex—What the heck is a trilobite, anyway?

[More laughter]

Graeme—A small furry animal.

Rusel—It's a relative of the llama, I'm sure. But, back to game design, tell me about how you come up with the puzzles?

Rob—I think I've just, by osmosis, gotten insight on basic kinds of puzzles and how suitable they are for our purposes. I've gained a lot of clarity, finding old logic puzzles, distilling, adapting, and modifying them for computer play.

Graeme—Well, one of the problems with *11th Hour* as well is in seeing the puzzle idea, but then getting it right. There're a lot of puzzles where we actually got something better than we anticipated. But, most of the time, it's a process of just going back and doing it again and again and again, you know, to get it working right.

Rusel—Some puzzles you could probably do in reality, you know, analog, but many are inherently electronic. When you think of a puzzle like that and you say, "Okay, I can see in my mind some concept here," how much do you really know how it's going to operate and how fun it's gonna be until you actually prototype it and try it out?

Rob—I think you get a feeling for how it's going to go. James (Yokota) just found a puzzle somewhere, another one similar to the switching bishops. I took a quick look at it, but didn't try to solve it or anything, but I could tell it had the potential to be a nice little gem. It had three pieces over here, and three pieces over there, and an empty space in the middle. And you know, right there, it's like, six pieces to swap, one empy space, and it's nice, elegant, and challenging. I haven't even played it, you know, but I like a good puzzle, and I can tell it's fairly easy, but hard enough.

Rusel—I guess the ones that are more confusing are the things like the Microscope and the Beehive, where you've got an idea of what it's all about, but when you start to play it, you find you don't even know how to proceed. Strategically, you can't explain it. You may be able to beat it or not, depending on how intelligent it is. You wrote the engine for all this, so you understand how it works. You understand the logic of the decision-making of the move.

Graeme—Mm, hmm.

Rusel—Even in that, did you understand that it would be fun, it would be playable? Obviously you had different levels of difficulty, as the Microscope sort of got a little easier to play if you went back to the Library and got hints.

Graeme—Most of the puzzles still are going to be a game. One puzzle that was never clear it was going to be a game was the Amazing Labyrinth (the mouse puzzle). And yet it turned out to me to be the most enjoyable puzzle in *The 11th Hour*. It's great. And actually, the logic behind that, on the part of the computer player, is completely different from any other logic that's ever been in this kind of game, really. Everything else followed it in a mad streak; it's way ahead. So it wasn't just "come up with that possible move from the position"—that just didn't work. It's almost a different approach to computer playing. It's also one of the hardest puzzles. I really don't know why.

Rob—I forget why that is. . . it started out where it was going to be a solitaire logic puzzle, where your object is go from this point to this point by switching the different shaped pieces to form a path. But then, Graeme worked on it, and I don't know, somebody else did and made it into an AI game which you play against Stauf.

Graeme—That's Patrick's work. Pretty high on the AI there.

Alex—You know, one of your programmers said that some of these were more difficult to solve than to code. . .

Graeme—[Laughs]

Rob—That would be the piano moving puzzle.

Alex—I just thought that was really interesting

Rusel—The other thing they said was that for some of them, they didn't know if there was a solution when they started. They would create a puzzle but they didn't really know if there was a solution.

Alex—No, not that you guys are picky, but that the programs themselves are exacting. Easier to code than to solve.

Rusel—Do you anticipate, like in *Clandestiny* and future products, puzzles with a really different, wild, new slant on puzzle-making?

Graeme—Yes.

[Pause]

[Much laughter]

Rusel—You keep pushing the envelope on these kinds of things.

Graeme—*Clandestiny* follows the formula that we derived in *7th Guest* and in *11th Hour* and we want to continue—it certainly seems to be popular. Therefore, it's something worthwhile continuing on our own. I think with each of the other games we have on the way, we're looking at experimenting on the wild side, trying to get closer to something a little bit different. You know, it's not the only formula out there, and certainly players shouldn't be forced to play these puzzle games every single time.

Rusel—Well, I don't want to get into too much detail about it now, but I know that I was really intrigued with *Dog Eat Dog* when Disney was doing it, and I was really happy that you guys took it. I'm excited that you're going to do something with it because I thought it was a wonderful concept. It's very different, and yet the potential for it, at any rate, in the way they were trying to do something, was wonderful—to create a totally different kind of game interaction and something that we can all kind of relate to.

[*Dog Eat Dog* was a project started by Disney Software, but never completed. It models a corporate work environment in which you try to climb the ladder to success.]

Rob—Yeah, for sure. We first heard about it on CNN, on a report from one of the trade shows. We knew there was going to be a report that included *7th Guest,* and *Dog Eat Dog* was one of the products in the report. We thought it sounded cool. Then we got a call, out of the blue, from a company that was leaving Disney, and they were developing this game. . .

Rusel—It was one of the most interesting products they had back then. I'm glad you're doing it.

Rob—Every time I mention the idea, people in the media go, "Oh really. . .? That sounds cool." They get it, you know, so it's a high concept thing. You don't really have to explain too much about it, for anyone to understand.

Alex—Bloopers. We want stories.

Rusel—Yeah, we want stories.

Alex—We heard some of the stories with film shoots—something about screaming in a graveyard. . . corpses in the trunks of cars. . . .

Rob—Did you hear about the guy, the actor, who was leaving the bar in downtown Jacksonville and could hear the screams of the actress doing a scene on location in the hills about a half mile away?

Alex—No, really?

Rob—It's not that far. And nobody called the police. Just like New York City, man.

Rusel—Yeah, I know; Jacksonville, New York. . . it's all how you interpret it.

Rob—That is scary.

Alex—Especially, you know, when you get over the visual similarities. . .

[Stunned laughter]

Alex—All the skyscrapers around here, in the fields.

Rusel—Now are there any really cool things that you guys put in here, Easter Egg type things, that maybe nobody knows about?

[Graeme bursts out in laughter. Right, as if they'd tell US those secrets.]

Rusel—Oh, stop laughing.

Rob—Well, you know, there's another password to get into the open house mode. You know about that already, huh?

Graeme—They're interested in other things. . .

Rusel—The ones that are harder to figure out. You know, a password to get into open house, I distrust, because I figure you may change it at the last minute. . . in the eleventh hour, so to speak.

Rob—[looks at Graeme] I guess we're not going to tell them anyway, huh?

Graeme—Actually, I don't think the open house mode is completely done. Even *7th Guest* has that one screen that comes up, where it was really nice. You had extra stuff. You could play the games, equivalent of an open house. But we could give you some stuff. Yeah.

Rob—Yeah.

Rusel—So, the issue will be that we will probably have a list of some of the things people have told us, that we have told Trilobyte we will not print, and once we have permission then we will let you tweak with it, and talk to you about it and we will say, "Could we print this, could we print that?" And you guys can decide what you feel comfortable with and what you don't.

Graeme—There's extra stuff on the actual CDs that we don't talk about in documentation or anything. But it's right there on the CD. Like there's a *Doom* WAD of *The 11th Hour* house, and all these WAD files that you can include in your windows and all these bitmaps for wallpaper. In the product itself, at one point there was going to be a lot of extra stuff, but towards the end of production those things tend to be squashed out. Maybe we'll have 'em back in.

[The *11h Hour Doom* WAD allows players of the game *Doom* to use the Stauf Mansion as a setting for their games of *Doom*.]

Rusel—I always figure, as a writer working with games, that I will never know all the secrets. Because even if programmers wanted to tell me, usually a lot of people have put different things in. . . .

Rob—Well, I don't know. As far as production goes, we could have put in some things.

Rusel—I was just asking if you knew of any yourself that were around.

Graeme—There is something in the player.

Rob—They know about it, they know it.

Rusel—Yeah?

Graeme—In the player? The game?

Rusel—I'd be interested. . .

Graeme—Oh, no. There's an extra game inside the player.

Rusel—An extra game?

Graeme—Yeah.

Rusel—No, we don't know about that.

Rob—[Laughs uncertainly]

Graeme—They don't know what I put in there. I've got all this stuff in there.

Rob—[Laughs out loud] No wonder you're being catty.

Graeme—Why do you think it's on so many CDs?

[Much laughter from all present.]

Rob—You're joking, now.

Graeme—[Pause] No. [Laughs maniacally] Once the game's out, I think I'll come forward with some of that stuff.

Rusel—Well, here's the deal. . .

[What follows is some wheedling and off-the-record negotiations that yielded what you see in the section titled, "Under the Floorboards."]

Alex—Are there any good stories about the making of this thing that you'd like to share?

Rob—Well, you know, it was such a long time ago.

Graeme—Yeah, three years. We didn't want to do it, and now that we've done it, we're really happy with it. It's been the hardest thing, I think, that both of us have ever worked on in our lives.

Rob—Aw. . .

Rusel—Harder than *7th Guest*?

Rob—Yeah. And *that* was hard.

Graeme—*7th Guest* was really hard. This was really, really hard.

Rusel—Why was *11th Hour* so hard—I mean, what was especially hard about it?

Graeme—Because we wanted to have it out as the quick sequel, to make money, and it ended up as the "be all, end all" product to beat *The 7th Guest* and beat where we were at. No one's even approached *7th Guest* in terms of what the public wants, or gameplay quality, or the technology, and each of those was bested easily in *The 11th Hour*. It made *7th Guest* look like the pre-quel to *The 11th Hour*. So, *The 11th Hour* is the main event. It's become a really, really great product.

Rusel—What's your favorite thing about the improvements you've made? What are you most happy about in those changes?

Graeme—Finishing them. [laughter] I don't know. Rob, what's the best change?

Rob—I don't know. I don't know. Oh . . . there are so many, it's hard to choose.

Rusel—What are the specific improvements that you think about, since *The 7th Guest*? What do you think is much better about *The 11th Hour*?

Graeme—It's not even similar. The product presentation is similar. The puzzles are more varied, I think, and that works well; I really like the video.

Rusel—The video's better. You knew which screen to use. . .

Graeme—Yeah, and technically it's much better, as is the creative design. You actually have reason this time to roam the house.

Rusel—You're happy with the basic presentation of the story and all that?

Graeme—Yeah, I think it works extremely well.

Rob—That's what I will be most interested to see, playing the game, when the excellence of the technology is apparent and the game play is proven. I just want to see how the story works within the game play. I'm too close to the product to judge. I'd like to hear people's comments and reactions to the story. There was a minimal amount of that with *7th Guest*; it was a little disappointing.

Rusel—You felt that people didn't really focus on the story much.

Rob—I don't blame them, you know.

Rusel—No, until I finished the game I didn't really understand it. And, when I did finish the game, toward the end, I started to get it. But, I really liked it, that's the thing. The reward of getting there was worth it.

Graeme—Yeah.

Rusel—I was the guy who liked it.

[Laughter]

Graeme—Yup, that's the guy.

Rob—It's a usual thing that people wonder about, and I think there'll be discussions, for example, about Martine Burden, how she died, what was that whole thing about. . . There are people now talking about *11th Hour* who're expressing curiosity about the story. And people are asking more about Stauf. It's amazing how Stauf has actually—for as little screen time as he actually has, he's become so popular.

Graeme—Yeah.

Rusel—Well you live with him throughout the whole game, though; you have him comment to you all the time. He becomes very familiar, and it feels like he's a part of everything you do.

Graeme—There were a lot of little touches, when the game (*7th Guest*) opened. Every time the game starts, Stauf says, "Welcome to my house", and right there, right from the very beginning, he welcomes you as part of it. And when you quit, "Come baaaaaack!" He really puts his stamp on that game!

Graeme—Yes, like down at Disney, looking at their animation system. You know, it's a great system. They use it to animate all their feature films with, and they've got exactly the same problems that we do. They've got bad frames in their animations, and it takes forever for animations to load up on the network, they have to wait four days for it to render. It's great.

[Much laughter from all]

We in many ways have a lot better tools than they actually have at Disney! I realize that theirs, of course, is at a somewhat larger scale, 'cause it's made for the big screen stuff. Everything's like 2K by 2K, or something like that. But that 2K by 2K takes a long time to load. And it doesn't go any faster down there than it does up here! It's really crazy.

Alex—Are you guys going to buy the Nunan House (the house used to model Stauf's house), and move into it?

Rob—Interesting idea.

Rusel—[To Graeme]: Well, you've got your shower.

Graeme—I don't like my shower, though.

Alex—Are you afraid it's going to fry you?

Graeme—Uh, yeah. Either that or it would transport me away to another shower, just on some other planet.

Rusel—Next time we come up here, we'd really like to see what you've done to your house. It sounds really fancy and stuff.

Graeme—Right. Well, my house is two weeks away from being done. It's been two weeks away from being done for about a year, now.

Graeme—One thing, you know, is that Rob and I have not taken lots and lots of money from *7th Guest* and made ourselves rich. We've increased our salaries a bit— we now pay ourselves!—But that's about the only thing. Everything has been about the company, what you see around you. The computers and the offices, and that stuff. That's what *7th Guest* has done for us.

Rob—[With mild sarcasm] My wife is pleased. "Yeah, I'm glad you're successful— when are you going to get a raise?"

Rob—We're not complaining and we're not big martyrs either, but we're not drivin' around in Testarossas or anything.

Rusel—Well, you do what you like to do, too.

Rob—We have fun, yeah.

Alex—Cruising those 45-mile-an-hour speed bumps in Medford, not quite like racing your Ferraris out there.

Rob—It would be nice to have one, though, on some of the country roads we have here!

Alex—I've got another question, which is that some of the aspects of the game were really bloody and violent and nasty and gross and graphic, AND you've also got sex in it. I'm not going to give away the play here, but just there are some soft moments where there's, like, skin and everything. I'm just wondering, did you consider that before you went into making the game? Was that something you thought, "Oh well maybe we can't do this, because it'll offend somebody?" Did you have to cut things out because they were too much?

Rob—Yeah, we shot some scenes different ways. This was what we referred to as the European version and the American version. We set out to make a strong story, but even the most adult versions we shot would have rated nothing more than than

PG-13, probably. R *maybe,* had it been released as a movie. I think even as it is people will react, "Ooh, there's blood, it's gory, there's violence." I don't do that myself, but there's intimation of all kinds of stuff.

Rusel—Well, when he's trying to pull the knife out!

Alex—Well, that's true to life, though. I liked it 'cause it's accurate.

Graeme—So you've had to take a knife out of someone?

Alex—I understand it's very difficult.

Graeme—Oh, OK. I didn't know that, myself.

[Laughter]

Rusel—I defer to her on all these body things.

Rob—So, that's something you understand from your—friend? Did I introduce Marie to you, Rusel?

[More laughter]

Rob—But that knife thing was a plot decision, you know. What happens is that, because he can't pull the knife out of the body, he is weaponless and can't kill his intended victim.

Alex—She's in the shower and she can't come out until—he has to leave, and without killing her.

Rusel—And, for some reason you couldn't figure any other way to kill him but with a knife, huh?

Alex—Couldn't end up bludgeoning him to death or anything, so—

Graeme—It's a natural, she's taking a shower. . . it could happen.

Alex—Oh, and my final question about gore is; Scruffy. She didn't know the part about the drowning kitten, did she? And, if that lion is in fact Scruffy's alter ego?

[Scruffy is the Trilobyte office kitty. A very relaxed feline.]

Alex—Is Scruffy taking questions?

Graeme—Scruffy has her own e-mail address. Just write to her and ask. Scruffy@tbyte.com.

Alex—Does she really?

Graeme—Yeah.

Rob—Yeah.

Alex—My cats will be online talking to Scruffy.

Rusel—Actually, was the lion something that you got out of some stock video or did you hire?

Graeme—No, we actually had one.

Alex—Wow. Where did you get the lion from?

Graeme—Well, on up the hill. . .

Rob—You wanted to hear a good anecdote about the 'making of.' We captured this lion. . .

Graeme—One of the scenes goes out of continuity—you know who's fault that is? Who messed that continuity point up? [Points at Rob]

Rob—Oh, uh, OK.

Graeme—Sort of, when she's facing the lion, and she's already scratched. Rob, right before that scene, goes, "It says in the script that she's going to be scratched up at this point. Could we scratch her up a bit in make-up?" Then they did the scene.

Rob—That's not true.

Graeme—Not true? Then what happened?

Rob—It's a good anecdote, but he's stretching it. As I recall, costuming said, "Hey, shouldn't Robin look a little disheveled and battered? After all, we want to imply that she's been trapped in this dark house for a while and has had some hellish exeriences." So they tore her shirt and added scratch marks. So people attribute the torn shirt and the scratches to the cat, and it looks like a continuity error. But, the cat was actually, just a little kitten. . . really.

Alex—A cub?

Rob—Yeah, it wasn't that old. It was scaled digitally to appear larger. An observant person might notice that as it leaps at her, it grows in size.

Alex—Did it come from the zoo, a person, a trainer, or what?

Rob—We tracked it down in the woods and caught it in a net. No, actually, we got it from a local wildlife preserve.

Rusel—And, no real animals were hurt in making of this, um . . .

Alex—Except Scruffy. Or Chuck. Chuck got hurt.

Rob—You want to hear an anecdote? There was a "making of" thing that was kind of funny. We were shooting at a motel and Chuck carried around dead bodies all over the place, right? So, he had all these dead bodies and somebody threw them in the back of the prop trailer and the feet of this fake corpse were hanging out with bloody sheets sticking out, and everything. And. . . the police showed up at the motel where we were shooting. They'd heard reports that somebody'd been done away with.

Rusel—This really happened?

Rob—Yep. They aren't used to us, movie-makin' up here.

Alex—Who had to explain to them that this was just acting?

Rob—I guess Howard, the production manager. He showed 'em the props.

[At this point the tape ran out and we flipped it over.]

Rob—We were just saying how easy this interview went, and now you want the final statement.

Alex—Yeah, just final thoughts, you know, how do you think *The 11th Hour* is gonna do?

Graeme—Oh, my gosh. . .

Rob—Actually that should be a question for you guys.

Rusel—Well, he already said, more than 70,000.

Alex—The trequel. Yeah, he said at least.

Alex—Will you ever—well, you're going to do another one, right? The trequel. . .

[Insane crack of laughter from Graeme]

Rusel—We already talked about that.

Rob—[Hesitantly] Uh. Well.

Alex—Yeah, but Rob wasn't here. Rob got committed. . .

Rusel—Right. Well, you're committed. You have no choice.

Rob—No, I mean—

Graeme—There'll be a 4, 5, 6 . . .

Rusel—This is going to be the 13th something, right? I think it'd work.

[Laughter]

Graeme—Maybe Robin will get the TV network Stauf promised her. . .

Rusel—When is there going to be a *7th Guest* movie?

Rob—Mmm. Uh.

Graeme—That's a good question.

Rusel—And, are there some talks going on, or anything like that?

Graeme—Yeah, there are some talks going on. It's Hollywood. It's extremely hard to tell. I really hope so. There's nothing I'd like more.

Rusel—I can imagine.

Rob—Jack Nicholson as Stauf.

Graeme—Clint Eastwood as Tad!

Rusel—Right, Jack as Stauf, that would be awesome, although Stauf is good as Stauf, too.

[More insane laughter from Graeme and Rob—Graeme gasping for breath as another demented thought comes into his head.]

Graeme—And, Tom Hanks as Julia Heine.

Alex—And, Robin Williams as everybody else?

Graeme—Some casting!

Rusel—Maybe it should be a movie with a choose-your-own ending, you know. Well, hopefully we can continue this interview sometime when we do a book on *Clandestiny* or something like that. We'll talk more. This will be an ongoing thing, you know. What is it, my dinner with Andre?

Under the Floorboards

11th Hour Easter Eggs

And finally. . . Here are some cool tricks and extras included with *The 11th Hour:*

WAD files

Yes, now you can play *Doom, Doom 2,* or *Heretic* (all from Id Software) in the Stauf Mansion! Use the special WAD files found on Disk #1 in the WAD directory. (Sorry, these WAD files will not be available in Germany.)

Sound Files

Can't get enough of Stauf's taunts? Check out the Z_WAV directory on Disk #1 for special sound files you can use. Add them to your Windows sounds if you dare!

Screen Images

The guys at Trilobyte decided you might like to have some cool screen images from *The 11th Hour.* Check out the Z_SHOTZ directory on Disk #1. View these images in any JPEG viewer, or convert them in a graphics program.

Screen Capture

Speaking of screen images, try this undocumented feature. Anywhere in the game that the cursor is showing, you can press F12 on your keyboard to snap a screen image in JPEG format. This won't work with the streaming video clips or the animation sequences. Sorry. But you can get great images of the house and of the puzzles. Amaze your friends!

Clock Navigation

Want a different way to get around the mansion? Here's a neat trick. It involves the grandfather clock found in the Foyer (near the Kitchen). Here's what you do:

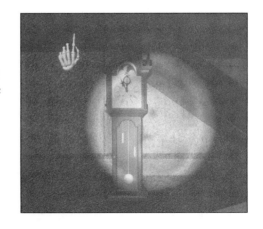

1) Go near the clock and click the cursor above and to the left of the clock. The picture to the right shows the exact position. The cursor will blink for an instant, indicating that you've found the correct spot.

Note: You must defeat the Knight Puzzle to open the Foyer before this trick will work.

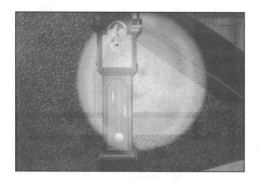

2) Position the eyeball cursor on the clock face and click to move closer to the clock.

3) Now position the cursor on one of the numbers on the clock face. The cursor will turn into an eyeball. Click on a number to move to another location. Notice that some numbers change locations after you get to certain modules of the game.

Guide to Clock Navigation

Click	Go To
1	Library
2	Top of Stairs (looking down) after 10pm to Music Room
3	Upstairs Hall (east side) after 9pm to Temple's Room
4	facing wall outside Music Room after 8pm to Game Room
5	Outside Library facing stairs after 8pm to Knox' Room
6	Bottom of stairs facing up after 8pm to Bathroom
7	Outside Bathroom facing stairs after 9pm to Attic
8	Outside Burden's Room facing stairs after 9pm to Room at the Top
9	Dutton's Room after 11pm to Nursery
10	Outside Dutton's Room facing door to Attic after 10pm to Doll Room
11	To Laboratory

Open House Access

Once you've completed the
game the first time, you'll
automatically gain access to
the Open House mode of
The 11th Hour. In Open
House mode, you can choose
Map Navigation by choosing
Map at the Game Book
screen. Then you can reenter
the game and simply click on
a location in the Map to go
there instantly. For instance,
in the picture to the right,
clicking on the Chapel takes
you there!

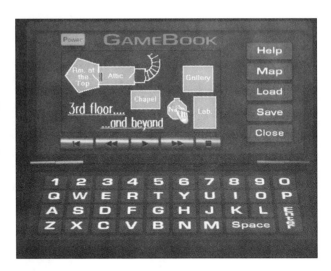

Pente Puzzle Difficulty

The final puzzle in the game is the Pente
Puzzle in the Doll House. The first time
you play Stauf, you get the first move and
Stauf doesn't really play his best. It's true.
But after you've completed the game once,
you may change your mind about who you
want to save. If you do try again, the game
gets harder. Stauf will get the first move,
which gives him an advantage. If you
defeat Stauf in this mode, he really gets
irritated, and if you go back for a third time, Stauf will not only get the first move, but
he'll be looking five moves ahead! Good luck!

Open House Codes

Yes, there is a special code you can enter at the opening skull screen of the game that
will take you instantly into the Open House mode. But no, we can't print it. Stauf has
threatened to cut out our tongues if we do. However, fans of *The Seventh Guest* may
remember the old password, Zaphod Beeblebrox (from *Hitchhiker's Guide to the
Galaxy*). This one doesn't work, but try it anyway. You'll get a special taunt from your
old friend and ours, Henry Stauf.